JACK HAYFORD

Sharpening
YOUR LEADING
EDGE

Moving From Methods to Mindset

SHARPENING YOUR LEADING EDGE by Jack Hayford
Published by Charisma House
A part of Strang Communications Company
600 Rinehart Road
Lake Mary, Florida 32746
www.charismahouse.com

Unless otherwise noted, all Scripture quotations are from the New
King James Version of the Bible. Copyright © 1979, 1980, 1982 by
Thomas Nelson, Inc., publishers. Used by permission.

Scripture quotations marked KJV are from the King James Version of
the Bible.

Scripture quotations marked NIV are from the Holy Bible, New
International Version. Copyright © 1973, 1978, 1984, International
Bible Society. Used by permission.

Cover design by Eric Powell
Interior design by Pat Theriault

Library of Congress Cataloging in Publication Data
Hayford, Jack W.
Sharpening your leading edge / Jack Hayford.
    p. cm.
Includes bibliographical references.
ISBN 0-88419-957-6 (hardback)
1. Pastoral theology. I. Title.
BV4011.3 .H38 2003
253—dc21

                2002154029

03 04 05 06 07 — 87654321
Printed in the United States of America

Section 3 Leading Through the Seasons
Putting an "Edge" on Celebration

[introduction] Warning: You May Be Disappointed!

I believe in this book. But hey, I wrote it!

However, there are hopeful signs for my believing it might be useful to you. I speak publicly to twenty to thirty thousand leaders a year (not counting media, TV, tapes, etc.), and they seem pleased. In fact, many testify to making gains in their work as they apply some of what I've said. (And, I'm sure they also apply some good stuff that others have given them, too.)

But I still decided to issue a warning on the front side here.

The reason is that while this *IS a book for leaders,* I think it isn't what some are looking for in a book on "Leadership."

I mean, lots of leadership books will tell you ways and means of dealing with *people.* Mine is more about dealing with *you.* Don't miss my point: Those other books *are* useful. They can and do help you with *methods.* But not always with *mindset.*

We all know *being* precedes any truly effective *doing*. And we've learned that the latter ought to flow from the former. *But what precedes being?*

> Don't be shaped by the world-mind, but be transformed by the renewing of your mindset...see God's will unfold.
>
> —ROMANS 12:2, AUTHOR'S PARAPHRASE

Whatever your skill set, mindset is the starting place. However your table's set, mindset is what will serve.

So, welcome to a set of articles focusing on *mindset.* Thinking about themes that will help shape a church leader's approach to such things as...

- [■] **Helping people you lead when their world shatters and philosophizing won't do**

- [■] **Focusing an approach to building men who can lead without alienating women around them**

- [■] **Celebrating life's season with warmth and vitality and with a perspective on their rich purpose**

- [■] **Finding pathways to self-discipline; forming patterns of thought that assure fruitfulness and durability**

- [■] **Leading the way at a time God's Spirit is seeking to unite the church beyond ethnic and Semitic separatism**

Those are for starters. And there's a good deal more. But for openers I wanted to define my target in this book so even if you are surprised, no one will be disappointed.

I don't think you will be.

—JACK HAYFORD

Section 1

Refusing to Be Blunted

Tempering My Perceptual "Edge"

Few things beleaguer or block the human soul more readily than perceptions that have been fixed in place by upbringing, culture—unless it is those laid in concrete by our theological prejudice or unperceived self-righteousness. Genetics, family influence, education or social influences are powerful in their restrictive capacities to our thought or vision. But doctrinaire and prejudiced lines of demarcation we view as "placed there by God Himself" are even more so (especially when the "lines" weren't His, even though we thought or said so).

This opening section presents responses to situations that required confrontation with status quo thinking, as well as refusing to excuse myself in the name of "avoiding the controversial" or in the mood of "leaving it up to others to answer." A leader needs to avoid being blunted by poor habits of thought. In contrast, allowing the fire of God's truth to temper the mind will sharpen perceptions by clarifying precepts. Read on.

Sharpening Your Leading Edge

Back to back chapters open our dialogue, chapters offering the leader an invitation to shape solid thinking in the face of conventional philosophical—even "sometimes" theological—thought. What help can a leader be when disaster strikes?

In sequence we consider the fact that a 9-11-01 event happens *every day* at the personal level of people around you. Moreover, earthquake shake-ups not unlike Northridge '94 shatter individuals whether seismic disasters hit them or not.

Every leader needs equipping on how to address circumstances that raise the question, "Why?" Better answers provide comfort and confidence where, of often, truth-and-worn ones tainted with human philosophizings only leave people in quandaries rather than answering questions.

For More...

In the wake of the San Francisco earthquake of 1989 and the Northridge quake of 1994, I brought assertive teaching that communicates biblical truth in the face of disaster—declaring the message of God's redemptive power and release through hope. The principles addressed in the two-audiocassette series *"Earthquakes and Disasters"* (SC213) speak to any natural disaster irrespective of its specific seismic or meteorological nature.

[chapter 1] A September 11 . . . of Any Kind

WITHIN hours following the events in New York and Washington and through the following two weeks, I served, as did others, in a bittersweet task. It was bitter by reason of the need, and sweet by reason of the opportunity to offer healing truth and prayer. Doors opened across our nation to speak into the lives of many—some only seeking comfort, others seeking some meaning in their torment amid the apparently meaningless tragedy.

I was invited to nearly a dozen radio and TV venues—local, regional and national. Network reporters and talk-show hosts ask hard questions in such moments. I was glad that, in most cases, they were sensitive enough not to require "sound bite"-size answers.

Reviewing the questions most frequently asked, I realized how often these same inquiries are thrown your way. Every leader faces situations in which he or she needs to address these themes either in local news media or with individuals we serve. Be it a national or global disaster, or a car wreck maiming or killing someone in your congregation, a myriad of questions inevitably surface. What follows addresses questions asked regarding September 11, but the "thought grid" involved is offered for what value it might serve in the face of any number of tragic situations.

These answers, while brief, are my effort at providing people—believers and unbelievers alike—with what I see as helpful, clear-thinking principles rooted in God's Word. I realize my responses may conflict with some, but I am troubled by the fact that even Christians often yield to ideas that, at most, are only philosophical answers flavored by theological prejudice or popular opinion.

Let me invite your consideration of the following. I hope the concepts may serve a future time, and I think that possibly, even yet, they might help you address issues related to the unthinkably demoniacal events we navigated only weeks ago.

Question No. 1: Was This a Judgment From God?

All sin exposes human beings to judgment, so perhaps it is

always wise to inquire into this at some point. However, I do not believe this is the right question to ask first, though evil or destructive things should prompt this honest personal inquiry: To what degree is my repentance—not that of others—being called for or overdue?

Plague, famine, war, disaster, tragedy and calculated evil are constant points of vulnerability to humanity by reason of our sin, sinning or outright godless rebellion, but it is deeply troubling to me to witness the inclination of some Christians to make a rush to judgment anytime something tragic or disastrous occurs.

Jesus addressed this human disposition in Luke 13:1–5, noting two things:

- That every one of us needs to repent to avert judgment

- That no one, in God's eyes, is deemed worthier of judgment than others

The terrorist attack on our nation (or any other visitation of human or hellish awfulness) calls believers more to identify with the brokenness and pain present among those impacted than to seize this as a platform to issue self-righteous denunciations of sin. Yes—sin does reap a bitter harvest.

Yes—America is a sinful nation. But, no—I don't believe God slashed New York and Washington apart in order to get even with America.

In speaking to a blinded, broken society, my understanding of God's present judgment relates to that which He visited long ago, on His own Son, when He dealt conclusively with all sin with unmeasured grace and redemptive power. When people are torn, I believe the church is to rise with love, comfort, service and redemptive hope. We are to demonstrate the Good Samaritan's example and contribute to the healing process of the broken rather than the religionists' separatism.

This is how Jesus taught neighborliness—with a definition requiring partnership in pain, not condescension toward those apart from God. I hold no casual attitude toward sin. But I fear some sincere believers hold too casual an attitude toward God's mercy—especially at times when people need to hear of it from us who have tasted His love.

Question No. 2: Why Does God Allow Evil Things to Happen?

In the face of horror, pain or evil's apparent success, a whole Bible answer will make clear that these things are neither acts of God nor willed by Him. "Proof-texting" philosophical opinions by referencing Job's struggle or by quoting Romans 8:28 out of context only perpetuates confusion.

The error that blames God for everything that happens in this world, or the old saying that suggests, "Well, God at least 'permitted' it, so it is His will," betrays a fundamental fact of Scripture: God's sovereign will is that human beings have a free will. What a person or group does with that freedom of choice only reflects His will to the degree they choose to come under the government of His will.

Further, besides being the fruit of sinfully willful humans, so much of evil's momentary victories are spawned in and spewed from hell—they are of satanic origin. When the existence of such malignancy manifests, never concede that God is somehow tolerant of evil or standing powerless before it.

Rather, affirming that His love does grant the power to choose good or evil, proclaim the even greater love He is ready to show, ever present to work redemptively and restoringly—ultimately overpowering the ability of evil's devices to succeed.

The Cross indicates the lengths to which God will go to

pursue breaking the power of the flesh and the devil by His love. God's present choice to not exercise His sovereign might—which could exterminate all participants in sin and evil in a split second—is matched to His sovereign love.

That love, in allowing humankind to choose its own course (including partnering with evil unto the most grotesque consequences), is neither indifferently passive nor aggressively active where horrible things happen. God is redemptively present—now and always—and He will continue to be until the day He shall consummate His long-suffering patience with demonic viciousness and human corruption.

Question No. 3: What Should Believers Do in the Wake of September 11?

An appropriate response by believers to tragedies such as those that took place in September is vital. Two things we should do:

1. **Engage in new levels of intercession. Pray for success in finding and executing the perpetrators of this recent evil.**

So many believers wondered, "Is it right to want to see retribution on those who did these things?" Because of the biblical truth that vengeance belongs to God alone (Ps. 94:1; Rom. 12:19), some mistakenly suppose this disallows human retributive action.

The Bible shows the opposite. Chapters 1–4 in the Book of Romans reveal that God wills human government as "His ministers" for executing His wrath and judgment upon evil. Thereby we understand 1 Timothy 2:1–3, directing the church's intercessory role for government and how God avenges evil through human instruments, and "a quiet and peaceable life" is gained in our society.

2. **Intercede for hope. Intercession is the most certain means for securing hope, recovery and—by God's grace—revival and restoration in the land.**

Jeremiah's prophecy of "a future and a hope" was spoken to a people also surviving the ransacking of a city (Jer. 29:11). Here is reason—beyond the ravaging of our nation's most symbolic city and the shattering of our nation's emotions— that we may prayerfully expect a visitation of God's grace across America. But it won't come without prayer's pursuit. Crises may stir desperation cries for God's help (and He mercifully answers even the most undeserving), but only sustained intercession will bring penetrating spiritual renewal.

The bottom line of September 11 is a call to faith and expectation—through prayer. We who lead must interpret the moment, then call God's people to faith-filled prayer and ministry.

Beyond all questions and our efforts at answers, I see God standing in the wings—not only available to comfort and heal America, but also to save and transform her. Join me in pursuing the faith-filled conviction that God is near and ready to meet us with great grace—great grace!

Jack Hayford, "A September 11...of Any Kind," *Ministries Today* (November/December 2001).

[chapter 2]   Earthquake: Judgment or Mercy?

IT was January 17, 1994—and it was horrifying in the San Fernando Valley area of Los Angeles! Two million people had their emotional world shattered, felt the impact of the indescribable, and most lived to taste the meaning of "post-quake trauma."

REFUSING TO BE BLUNTED—TEMPERING MY PERCEPTUAL "EDGE"

Sixty-one didn't live. Their trauma ended within seconds or minutes of the Northridge earthquake—sixteen of them the victims of a pancaked apartment building that appeared in newscasts to have had nothing happen to it, since the top two stories seemed to be sitting in a normal position. The problem was...another floor was sandwiched in the twelve to eighteen inches between the second floor and the first. It is still an awe-striking memory to reflect on if you were there. The expert seismologists at the California Institute of Technology were mystified about how to measure this "two-impulse" shaker. They finally calculated a Richter scale magnitude of 6.8, although they acknowledged the "ground action" near the epicenter was equivalent to the magnitude of a 9.1 quake (in my neighborhood, the equal of an 8.3). But there was something more puzzling than the matter of measurement when you seek to gauge the response of the body of Christ in other parts of the nation.

As bewildering as the aftermath of the earthquake was for those of us living in that part of Southern California, even more puzzling was the speed with which Christians outside the quake zone passed their spiritual judgment on the event. Faxes and letters, radio and television commentary, individuals phoning to deliver their "word" with seeming omniscience—the hue and cry rang out: *"Los Angeles is getting what it's long deserved. God has judged the city!"*

At the same time, thousands of spiritually committed, morally sensitive, biblically centered pastors and church workers here were trying to comfort the bereaved, pacify the terrified, feed and house the hungry and homeless, partner with relief agencies to service the aftermath and come up with messages from God's Word to nourish and reassure His devoted, faithful sheep, who were as devastated by the tragedy as the most corrupt sinners.

With aftershocks continuing by the thousands, giving rise to sensations of repeated horror every time, what was a pastor supposed to say—to teach—in such circumstances? Indeed, what does the Bible say about earthquake disasters? Are they natural seismic events, or are they divine judgments from God?

Mercy Over Judgment

After the quake, I received requests for radio and television interviews right and left, all wanting an answer to this very question. The fact that the quake centered within blocks of the porno-flick hub of the world—where 90 percent of the

REFUSING TO BE BLUNTED—TEMPERING MY PERCEPTUAL "EDGE"

filth-films are spun out to the nation—seemed to some interviewers to verify all charges of "Judgment!"

"What do you think, Pastor Hayford?" (Careful now, Jack. Too much grace at this point will subject you to the scorn of every legalist and to the suspicion of most others who have concluded that "nothing good" can come out of a corrupted "Nazareth" named Los Angeles.) But here's the answer I gave—possibly one to consider whenever any of us are tempted to rush to judgment when we hear of disasters.

First, every natural disaster *is* a judgment of sorts. According to the Word of God, this world—which God described as "good" after He created it—was drastically damaged as a result of the curse sin brought into its fabric. Even many believers are uninformed of the fact that a good deal more than just mankind "fell" as a result of sin's impact on our planet. Because of sin, our whole world, which God fashioned in desirable wholeness, was broken, and it continues to this day to be liable to every order of natural disaster.

Second, as to whether God personally "sent" the Northridge earthquake, I doubt it. If the almighty God were intending to shatter Los Angeles for its sin—a judgment of which we are more than deserving—He certainly miscalculated His timing, for there were amazing signs of abounding mercy everywhere. God's hand of providential intervention—saving life—was far more prevalent in this quake than was His judgment. Either that or His watch was broken. By striking at 4:31 A.M. on a holiday, the quake missed multitudes who could have been far more efficiently "judged" thirty-six hours later when people would have been present in droves at the locations so dramatically destroyed.

Third, I would assume that in the aftermath of such an awesome reminder of our human frailty, fragility and finiteness, any thinking person would reevaluate their lifestyle and relationship with the Almighty. Because yes! We are a sinful culture. Yes! We deserve God's judgment. And yes, it's time for everyone—from pornographers and homosexuals to loveless religionists and priggish Pharisees—to repent! And don't think for a minute that God's mercy-in-the-midst hasn't garnered healthy responses.

Biblical Facts

Hear me, please; these recollected conclusions are not the fruit of sentimental babblings of "grace" for so cheap a reason as having suffered at the scene. I wasn't simply "feeling generous toward fellow sufferers." More than noting the

REFUSING TO BE BLUNTED—TEMPERING MY PERCEPTUAL "EDGE"

aforementioned ongoing bitter fruit of the curse consequent to the Fall of man, I looked at biblical facts in cases of earthquakes:

1. There is not one recorded earthquake in the Bible that was characterized as "judgment." The key seismic events in the Scriptures seem to signal divine visitations of grace. Any such "judgment" that does occur eventuates in the blessing of those who believe. For example, the quake at the Cross, the one at the Resurrection and the ultimate "big one" in the Book of Revelation each reveal two things: 1) a breaking of the power of evil, and 2) a furtherance of God's program of redemption. (A close study of the one text that seems to differ—Isaiah 29:6—reveals that it too supports this proposition.) All together, it appears that earthquakes are "grace-quakes" on mankind's behalf far more than judgments of God poised in fury against people.

2. The often-cited case of Sodom and Gomorrah noted almost gleefully by some who see events in Los Angeles as a parallel (and thereby a vindication of their own standard of righteousness) speaks to this subject. Its message: "If a natural disaster is a judgment, expect total devastation, not token destruction." When I was asked about the possibility that the Northridge pornographers were "getting theirs" at God's hand, I responded, *"Any* of us have big-time reasons to repent. All I know is that the porn business was back at work within a week—Sodom and Gomorrah weren't. There's a message there somewhere."

Now, in saying all of this, I'm not denying that God has the judicial right or the sovereign might to wreak any judgment He wants. We all deserve the worst.

I'm also not arguing against the propriety of outright repentance, heart-searching or any other order of introspection and self-judgment that should occur when our world is turned upside down by flood, quake, winds or seas. Those are valid issues that ought to be kept in view. But with them, I believe there are larger issues we tend to overlook when we have too great a readiness to lambaste with our accusations those persons and situations already beaten up by tragic circumstances.

Rallying the Flock

I didn't change my standard of righteousness in the post-quake season here in Los Angeles. I haven't forgotten that the wages of sin is death and that it's a fearful thing to fall into the hands of an angry God. These are changeless truths that call for humility, reverence for God and walking softly in righteous obedience to His throne. In sharing with my own congregation, I affirmed these holy things, but I shepherded shattered sheep by noting other *healing* truths as well:

1. I preached on Jesus' words in Luke 13:1-5 about non-selective judgment. We studied the implications of His presence and response to the seismic event that contributed to the tempest on the Sea of Galilee. (See *seismos* [Greek] in Matthew 8:24.)

2. I called God's flock to rally from their own pain to serve those who suffered around us. With the help of a host of you from across the nation, we were able to serve tens of thousands with food and hundreds with shelter—and we were just one congregation among many who rose in Jesus' name to show His grace and mercy.

3. I focused my people's attention on the incredible numbers of providential "interventions" that took place—stories of God's merciful sparing of life and property with clear signs of angelic activity during the quake. I urged them not to feel guilty for such blessings, even though there were some who didn't experience the same preempting mercy. Our call is to "rejoice with those who rejoice," as well as to "weep with those that weep" (Rom. 12:15).

4. I openly shared my feelings of post-quake trauma and discovered that my honesty about my fears helped multitudes deal with their own pain and struggles.

Hands Off

Perhaps it's a time for all of us to remember that God isn't in the business of dealing out Sodom-and-Gomorrah judgments right now. Without doubt, they are due to our race in due time. But in the meantime, let us remember—Calvary was His judgment focus; the "shake-up" there two millennia ago provided grounds for an ongoing mercy still prevailing above all human sin and failure. Since that time, He's called us—first and foremost—to broadcast "grace unto salvation" on the basis of that once-for-all work.

At the end of time, things will be different. But until then perhaps it's wisest to keep our hands off the trigger of "quick-draw" pronouncements of judgment when anyone, anyplace meets disaster.

> **For God did not send His Son into the world to condemn the world, but that the world through Him might be saved.**
>
> **—John 3:17**

Jack Hayford, "Earthquake: Judgment or Mercy?" *Ministries Today* (May/June 1994): 8–9.

Sharpening Your Leading Edge

Surrender is hardly a leadership word, at least in the mindset of society in general. But in the processes of God's kingdom it is a foundational term. In fact, there are no pathways to triumph or victory apart from having learned "surrender"—by God's definition.

Within the ebb and flow of all human relationships the same principle applies. A leader gains leadership influence with people *not* by conquest, but by service; *not* mandate, but by wisdom and understanding. The fountainhead of both is found in the Cross of Jesus Christ, where—in a matter of a few hours—not only is human redemption provided, but the answer to how life's most difficult times may be handled.

A lifetime of setting the pace for others has taught me that periodic requirements will be faced by a leader that give him or her no space for self-assertion or domination—only surrender. Discerning when those times are and how to handle them will not only bring triumph beyond surrender, but also expanding influence by reason of the divine law: When the *sowing* unto death is submitted unto, the *growing* unto life will be realized (John 12:24).

For More...

This chapter is adapted from a book in which I have explored seven keys to handling difficulties. *How to Live*

Through a Bad Day is a concise, step-by-step assessment of Jesus' words from the Cross—the "bad day" usually called Good Friday.[1] Its brief format makes it uniquely suited to give to people you deal with—assisting them with their tough times; its readable content makes it easily assimilated and applied.

I made this adaptation from *How to Live Through a Bad Day*, my book with Thomas Nelson Publishers, not only to address a crucial leadership issue, but also in order to acquaint leaders with my book as a resource to assist counseling and comforting people they lead who are struggling.

[chapter 3] When It's Tough to Surrender

WHEN you come to the end of any season that's been hard, tough or heartbreaking, it's usually as difficult to conclude as it has been to live. The end of such a time so often becomes the start of a soul's long night of restlessness, reliving the struggle and reexperiencing its pain.

But into such days, moments or seasons of the soul, Jesus' closing words from the Cross speak a principle of discipleship laden with wisdom: "Father, into Your hands I commit My spirit" (Luke 23:46).

There is something preciously sublime about Jesus' final words from the Cross. Though sometimes overlooked, falling as they do in the wake of Calvary's grand pronouncement—"It is finished!"—their message points the way to wisely conclude any bad day, any trying experience: Place it into the hands of God and leave it there.

The Savior's words demonstrate a colossal act of trust, surrendering His control of life into the Father's hands. While an hour before He was torn with the agony of abandonment—"Why have You forsaken me?"—now He concludes this day with a declared confidence in the Father, these final words saying, "I'm letting go and placing everything into Your hands." At Calvary's finale, Jesus gives us a lesson on how to live through life's trials.

More Than a Bad Day

Trina sat in my office, the picture of composure. An attractive woman in her early forties and the wife of a successful physician, she was the essence of social grace and cultural sophistication. But there was nothing of snobbishness or the superficial—Trina was a devoted servant of the Savior.

She had come to Christ several years before, and her growth of years in Christ was marked by humility, as surely as her background evidenced regal dignity. But Trina's husband had never come to the Lord.

I had seen Walt in church a few times and met him once. Two things were clear. First, he had a genuine respect and almost reverent regard for his wife's faith. He recognized she possessed a dimension of life bringing something valuable to their home and marriage.

But there was a second thing—the evidence of that subtle deception that suggests to an otherwise reasonable mind: "You don't need this (this Savior, Jesus). If you ever open to Him, it will cost genuine transformation, and you don't want to stop being who you really are, now, do you?"

It was in Walt's face—that fundamental dishonesty of a "knowing" soul being dishonest with God...and knowing that, too.

But on this day when Trina asked to see me, she was direct and to the point. "Pastor Jack, I want to ask more for your prayer than for your counsel. It relates to something I feel convinced I am to do. I don't want to seem to have taken leave of my senses, but I don't know anyone I can tell—nor do I plan to tell anyone else other than Lisa, my closest friend.

"You've met Walt," she continued, "and you know what a fine man he is. And though he isn't a Christian, he has openly admitted to me that he knows he should give his heart to the Lord.

"Pastor, I believe you know I am not the nagging, religious wife-type. By God's grace, I believe I've obeyed God's Word in living and loving like a wife should—and Walt acknowledges this. He often expresses his gratefulness for my care for and attentiveness to him."

I braced myself. I was ready for the point to be made—one all too frequently surmised and asserted today by Christian spouses who say, "I've done everything I can, and I'm tired of trying; I want to get a divorce from my unbelieving wife/husband."

But instead, I was spun for a complete loop when Trina continued the explanation of her prayer request.

When Life Unravels

"Pastor Jack," she said, lowering her eyes in slight embarrassment, "I don't want to seem at all inappropriate to you, nor make this any more awkward for me than it already is. But frankly, Walt is having an affair.

"I discovered this in finding some medication he left in the cabinet—medicine for the treatment of venereal disease. When I confronted him about it, he admitted both to an affair and to having contracted the disease from this other woman."

She paused, and I inquired, "Presuming you and he have been pursuing your normal sexual relationship, how did

Walt respond to your finding this out, seeing as he is now exposing you to the same disease?"

"He was a mix of shame and humiliation," Trina replied. "He made no self-defense and apologized, yet he also asserted he couldn't promise he wouldn't yield again to the same temptation."

She teared slightly, embarrassed but retaining control. I waited, then invited her to continue as she felt able. To my amazement, she was not requesting permission to exit her marriage, but had come to request abiding prayer covering for her own physical protection.

"You see, Pastor Jack, I believe I have every right to either walk away from Walt or to at least deny him bedroom rights until he is, first, cleared of the infection and, second, done with the woman."

I nodded my agreement, but she wasn't done. "But, Pastor, I also believe the Lord is calling me to demonstrate my love for Walt in a way that will make an inescapable statement about God's love for him. Pastor, I believe I am to remain sexually available to him, even though it could be at the risk of my life."

She further described having found a magazine with photos of naked men in pornographic interplay and wondered if Walt might be dabbling in ways that could even lead to her being exposed to AIDS.

"I know it's radical, Pastor," Trina continued. "And I hope you will understand my decision as neither some fanatical foolishness or a desperate act of clutching for my husband's affection. But I see the problem simply as this: Walt is a horribly blinded soul.

"My hope is that by loving him as Jesus loves us—'while we were yet sinners, Christ died for us'—my action, however self-risking, might shake him awake and help him come to Christ."

Into God's Hands

I was as moved as I have ever been by one person's sense of marital commitment.

Nothing—I emphasize it, nothing—in the Bible requires this kind of caring; indeed, Trina had full biblical license to walk away from Walt. But she chose as she did, and I still remember it with amazement, for nothing in my experience has ever manifested a more dramatic commitment to self-sacrificing love.

As I prayed with her that day, Jesus' words rose to my lips, "Father, into Your hands we commit Trina's life." She had chosen a path of trust and surrender in the midst of a horrible situation, and the Father's hands were the only ones that could shield and secure her.

The facts are that a year or so later, Walt left Trina. He chose a promiscuous and perverted life instead of Christ—and lost the devotedly marvelous woman he had as his wife.

And Trina? She was never infected, though she continued as her husband's lover and faithful wife until the day he announced he was leaving. She kept her life constant in Christ, and though I haven't seen her for years, she still has a strong relationship with her children and with her Savior.

I have never proposed Trina's "surrender" as a model to anyone, but it certainly strikes an opposite chord to the readiness with which many Christian believers will walk away from their marriages today, saying things have "gone bad." And I note her story here, not as a model for behavior in such situations, but as a model of surrender in dealing with bad days—or worse—by surrendering absolutely everything to God.

This is livable reality for all of us, because a marriage isn't the only arena in which we are often called to live through "bad days." There are dozens of life issues that call us to follow Jesus' pathway in living through tough times, issues that are seldom as quick to pass as we would wish and that always call us to the Cross and to hear the Savior's words again, "Into Your hands I commit."

Committing ourselves into His hands may be the key for some of us to enter a new day—or new year—with new-found expectancy, notwithstanding the "bad" behind us.

For Jesus, the end of it all finally was revealed in a resurrection. For you and me—where "surrender" is truly made—there's full reason to expect precisely the same.

Jack W. Hayford, "When It's Tough to Surrender," *Ministries Today* (January/February 2002): 18–19.

REFUSING TO BE BLUNTED—TEMPERING MY PERCEPTUAL "EDGE"

Sharpening Your Leading Edge

On a planet that communication and transportation have shrunk until the whole world is next door to every one of us, leaders must lead the way as reconcilers amid human estrangement. Racism and discrimination, prejudice and inter-ethnic strife, not only are everywhere—but they have tainted the soul of every human being. We are all subliminally, if not directly, educated to view certain cultures with favor and others with disdain.

Into this global problem God has placed the church—and we who lead in it. If there is going to be any healers, anywhere—any reconcilers who rise in force—they must be found among God's people. This article is simply a signpost pointing toward a posture of spirit—one leaning as far as possible to embrace, one reaching to touch as deeply as possible to heal.

For More...

There is a remarkable resource available to the whole body of Christ through PromiseKeepers in Denver, Colorado. Ask for information on "The Eight Biblical Principles of Reconciliation."[2]

My audio-video-booklet material *Outracing the World* was born of the time I faced the decision to lead our church toward "trans-ethnicity" so we could embrace the whole of our city rather than lead our people to the geographical fringe of the city, where becoming a multiethnic congregation would not be necessary.

[chapter 4]

Let's Race to Reconcile

ENTERING the twenty-first century, it is profoundly clear on the social and spiritual landscapes that racial issues are large on the agenda. There's not a single pastor—no matter how rural or ethnically landlocked his or her place of service may be—who isn't having to answer questions or deal with issues in this category. It shouldn't surprise us—it is large on God's agenda, too.

Multiethnic conflicts and concerns are included in our Lord Jesus' prophetic summary of the last days: "Nation [the Greek word is *ethnos,* meaning a race, ethnic group or nation] will rise against nation, and kingdom against kingdom" (Matt. 24:7). In those concise words, the Savior revealed that racial tensions are an inescapable reality destined to increase in complexity as the end draws nearer.

This puts the matter squarely at a leader's door. We'll either seize the moment as a doorway for spreading the good news, or else we'll shortly find ourselves out of touch with the times—with the door slammed on our access to many of the peoples of our communities.

In every town today are a variety of people groups—all to be loved, understood and touched in Jesus' name. I can't afford to let our congregation's meeting place become a sanctuary of retreat from the realities of one of the world's greatest needs. The Rodney King beating and trial, right in my hometown, put the charge on more tables than those of Los Angeles Christians. Every flock in North America today has to face decisions as to attitudes and actions on the subject of discrimination, racial profiling, latent dispositions of anger and the lurking presence of racism in more places than we care to identify. You and I lead people who are uneasy about the eventual outcome of these issues—good people, but ones who struggle with unresolved racial issues of their own, such as:

[■] **Fears—subliminal if not conscious**

[■] **Prejudices—deep, though often unperceived**

[■] **Undefined spiritual questions—with a deepening sense that the world's answers often aren't solutions at all**

Facing tomorrow, we need a clear-headed grasp of the Lord's

strategy for addressing these issues today. Through the light and insight of God's Word, we need to lead our people into discerning intercession and decisive reconciling action. As a pastor I need to lead my flock beyond social commentary to divine revelation, and thus, past being mirrors of our racially divisive and opinionated culture. I first came to my most serious sense of pastoral responsibility on this subject over a decade ago.

Although God had been helping me process my own unperceived "systemic racism" from early in my ministry, I hadn't said much from the pulpit. In fact, I'm of a generation of evangelical-Pentecostal extraction that has tended to describe racial matters as "political" and therefore outside the proper concern of the church. But when the riots following the Rodney King trial exploded in my city, I was jolted to new awareness and struck by a deep conviction I still hold—only God's people hold the key to releasing true reconciliation in the world. I realized that if I didn't teach and lead my people to be reconcilers in our community, I've misread the Great Commission no matter what the size of our missions offering. I faced up to the call that we not only are to "go into all the world" with the gospel, but we also are assigned to live it out locally.

The place of racial sensitivity and reconciling concern is shown in a variety of biblical episodes I had hardly recognized until my city was torched by hatred:

- [■] **Jesus' racially pregnant story of the Good Samaritan (Luke 10:25–37)**

- [■] **The resolution of ethnic strife in the supposedly "ideal" first church (Acts 6)**

- [■] **The Holy Spirit's confrontation of Peter's racial prejudice (Acts 10)**

- [■] **The Jerusalem Council meeting that officially ended the Gentiles' second-class status (Acts 15)**

These examples are capped by the apostle Paul's message of reconciliation in 2 Corinthians 5:9–21 and his eloquent declaration in Ephesians 2:11–22. With such passages underscoring the broadband intention of God's reconciling work in us, and our consequent assignment to be reconcilers in our world, I have a fresh realization that the reconciling, serve-the-city role of the body of Christ is my community's only hope. We as the church need to model behavior that demonstrates the power of Christ to surmount systemic racism.

As you might willingly turn a page in your own ministry

agenda hereby, allow me to caution you. I've learned we need to "Look out!"

1. **"Look out!" because the adversary will seek to distract you from your primary role as a Spirit-filled curer of souls into becoming a mere social commentator regarding the 6 o'clock news.**

2. **"Look out!" because the spirit of the world will seek to reduce your heart and mind to the size of those who forget that love alone can win, for it alone can cast out the fear that divides peoples.**

3. **"Look out!" because those we lead will be tempted merely to mouth opinions about events rather than pursue *both* faithful intercession and discerning social action.**

To help us leaders forward—and do so with wise discernment—an increasing number of resources are available, pointed toward awakening the church's sensitivity to its healing role amid racial division. Also, seek to make friends with African American, Hispanic, Native American and Asian leaders in your community. Ask them to help you gain a greater sense of what it means to be disenfranchised or marginalized in our society.

Such resourcing can help us see how our unwitting neglect of our brothers and sisters in other ethnic communities has breached a trust. Regaining that trust will require initiative on our part—going to the inner city to share resources redemptively and finding ways to serve social need. This not only will build trust with believers of other ethnicities, but it also will enable the world to see credible evidence of Christlike care.

The Last Barrier

In my view, this awakening of unity—superseding our racial and denominational boundaries—is calculated by the Holy Spirit to break the last barrier to the great and final harvest.

As my friend Bishop Charles Blake, one of today's foremost African American leaders, has said, "Genesis 11 reveals that God, in observing a sinful host united in arrogance and pride, said, 'Nothing they propose to do will be withheld from them.' If that's His assessment of a united people joined to oppose His throne, think what He might do in our cities when His children—bonded from every ethnic group—unite to serve His purposes!"

Fellow shepherd, I believe the Holy Spirit is poised for a new thrust that will shake the current society. While the world futilely gropes for answers to race-riddled strife, the solution lies in our hands. If we'll respond to the Spirit's prompting, there is reason to expect Him to unveil a world-changing model of reconciliation through Christ's body.

Let's join hands with Him—and each other.

Jack Hayford, "Let's 'Race' to Reconcile," *Ministries Today* (January/February 1996): 18–19.

Sharpening Your Leading Edge

Consistent with the summons in the preceding chapter, I draw your attention as a leader to what has proven history's longest-term recurrence of prejudice: animosity against Jews—anti-Semitism. Peculiarly, unperceived insensitivity exists in large segments of the believing church and impacts leaders by failing to alert us to the possibility for wise and gracious action.

A present awakening is occurring, but there are still many who are mired in the past, and murky thinking blunts the edge of their ability to lead with discernment in these particularly significant times. In the wake of the increase of anti-Israel, anti-Jew attitudes evidenced in much of the world, let every leader of faith allow the words that follow to sharpen perception…and responsiveness.

For More…

Don Finto, pastor emeritus at Nashville, Tennessee's renowned Belmont Church, has written insightfully on this theme in his book *Your People Shall Be My People*.[3]

See Dan Juster's books *Israel, the Church and the Last Days* and *Jewish Roots*.[4]

Consider my recent two-tape series, "Why Stand With Israel Today?" It provides historical insight with present action steps believers should consider, also resolving the question as to how we may demonstrate pro-Israel action, yet *never* be or be seen as anti-Arab. (God has great promises for that portion of Abraham's seed, too!)

Broad informational resources can also be found at www.istandwithisrael.org or by e-mailing maozisrael @maozisrael.org.

[chapter 5] Discerning the Times and Messianic Ministries Today

THE ever-increasing intensity of strife in Israel and the Middle East today is fraught with prophetic significance. In the middle of it all is one huge issue too seldom perceived by leaders at the depth necessary to wisely inform and guide those they lead in times like these. The danger is more than simply failing to teach "Israel in Biblical Prophecy." That subject is present in profusion in most Bible-believing circles. But serious miscalculation if not outright unawareness abounds concerning global anti-Semitism, its low-grade presence in the historic church, the Holy Spirit's moving and work today in Israel itself, and the general issue of Messianic Jews—how today's church does and will relate to them.

I cannot too strongly urge believers who hold leadership roles—in the church and beyond, in business, politics, education and industry—to secure a balanced perspective on this watershed subject. What happens around this matter is at the cusp of everything pertinent to "last times" and the culmination of history as we know it. Thus, I offer the following biblical and historical review, providing a resource for understanding this timely circumstance—especially our call to relate to the prophetic and uniquely difficult ministry being pursued by the Messianic Jewish community.

It is "timely," to say the least. A century-long move of the Holy Spirit has been fulfilling the Ezekiel 37 "dry bones" vision, and a spiritual harvest is afoot among God's ancient, chosen people. Prophetic developments in Israel and among global Jewry ignite any thoughtful soul witnessing God's sovereign hand at work regathering "the lost sheep of Israel." Their regathering to "The Land" is probably the single most significant sign of the nearing of Jesus' Second Coming.

From Herzl and the birth of the Zionist vision (1890s–1917), to the horrors of the WWII Holocaust as six million European Jews were slaughtered in the Nazi death camps (1939–1945), to the founding of the modern State of Israel (1948), ongoing events have kept Israel in the international spotlight for a hundred years. Whether people recognize it or not, God is trying to get the world's attention.

A Mixed Response

Christian response to these events has varied widely. Many show unawareness and passivity, knowing little history or biblical prophecy. Others reveal interest and passion, but not always with discernment in their response or efforts. But for me, a basic understanding of a few key concepts sharpened my perception, helping me respond to the Holy Spirit's renewing and reviving ministry in this regard.

I came to realize that what God is doing among Jews and in Israel needs to be seen as being as much a "renewal" as the Spirit's revitalizing the church in such arenas as worship, the fullness and gifts of the Holy Spirit and the ministry of the believer. I began including some of the following in special teaching occasions and found people are helped—made better by seeing God's present purposes in Israel and among Jews—while also clearing their thinking about *Messianic ministry.*

To begin, "Messianic ministry" is relatively new terminology used today by most who seek to touch Jewish people with the gospel. Their outreach is commonly assailed by the Jewish religious community and thus by the press, accusing "Messianics" of *proselytizing* and attempting to steal Jews away from their Jewishness. However, Messianic evangelism is clear in its focus and message, seeking only to invite Jews to faith in their Redeemer, *without becoming any less Jewish.*

Misgivings and Misfirings

It's that last phrase that bewilders many—both Christians and Jews—a bewilderment that often breeds resistance to Messianic ministries. As I travel, speaking with leaders and, in general, feeling the pulse of the larger body of Christ, I am surprised at the frequency I encounter *both* misgivings and misfirings concerning ministry toward Jews.

The *misgivings* are found among sincere believers who are problemed through unawareness of key concepts undergirding Messianic ministry. The *misfirings* are the often sorely misguided "shots at saving Jews" taken by equally sincere believers whose absence of seeing the historical context of Jew/Christian relations boomerangs their intended "love for the Jews" into being seen as a crusade against them. These believers end up shooting themselves in the foot. The rejection they meet attempting to "spread the gospel of Jesus Christ" or seeking to "convert" or "complete" Jews too often leads to feelings of being "persecuted for righteousness' sake." The fact is, their approach is too

REFUSING TO BE BLUNTED—TEMPERING MY PERCEPTUAL "EDGE"

often dominated by ignorance, however innocent, and even a *few* points of review regarding Messianic ministry might have helped. Let me suggest those points that have helped me.

Points of Review

1. Messianic ministry does not begin with *excitement*, but with *exposition*. It is predicated on the Bible's revelation that God has never forgotten nor rescinded His timeless covenant with Israel/Jews. (See Romans 9–11.) Many Christians are not aware that a powerful residue of anti-Semitism present in sixteenth-century Reformers shaped a theological stance toward the Jews, one that dictates against sensitivity needed in today's environment. It is worthwhile to gain at least an elementary grasp of this issue and its resolution.

2. There is a distinct need for understanding and being sensitive in terminology. For example, the very term *Messianic* for this ministry is a strategic choice—one that peculiarly often faces criticism by Christians who don't realize how objectionable to Jews such words as *church, Christian, conversion* or even Jesus' name have become. To many Jews, the word *Christian* is weighted with negativism often completely unknown to or misunderstood by evangelical believers. Yet, whether we feel it is fair or not, these Jewish feelings are fully understandable when we see the following facts of

history as the majority of Jews do—thus shaping their view of Christians and Christianity:

- The Crusaders (during the eleventh and twelfth centuries), formally commissioned by Rome to drive "the infidel Muslims" from the Holy Land, just as readily killed Jews—by the thousands—for the same reason.

- Hosts of Jews were killed by the official church during the Spanish Inquisition (during the fourteenth and fifteenth centuries) because they would not convert to Christianity "on demand."

- For centuries, most Christians dubbed all Jews as "the Christ killers," and generations of children were taught anti-Semitic attitudes as a deserved retribution.

- The Protestant Reformation included no reform of the above attitudes; in fact, Martin Luther himself, in the spirit of the times, wrote with deep animosity against Jews.

- The Nazi Holocaust—targeting the extermination of the Jewish peoples—was spawned in a nation that was nominally "Christian," and meanwhile, most "Christian" nations around the world did virtually nothing to stop the slaughter (including the United States).

5. To the average Jewish mind, these events define the "Christian" attitude toward Jews, and thus the idea of "becoming a Christian" is readily defined as betrayal of one's own people and a renouncing of one's ethnic origin and history. Thus, since *Christ* literally means "Messiah," and since *the Messiah* is still a Person longed and hoped for by multitudes of Jews, those seeking to communicate God's love to today's Jew refer to themselves as "Messianic"—of or concerning the Messiah—rather than as "Christian."

4. Another key term, obviously essential in Messianic ministry, is the name of Jesus. Few contemporary Christians are aware of how sorely distorted the English name of our Savior—"Jesus"—has become, *both* by the failures of history we've reviewed as well as the corruption of His name and its meaning in the Jewish culture. The name *Yeshua* is the literal Hebrew equivalent of Jesus' name, and it is used in all Messianic ministry today. This too is often objected to by some who brand the practice "cultish" (though such a charge would never be brought against a Hispanic ministry for pronouncing Jesus *"Hay-soos"*).

5. Finally, the times demand removing the objections Messianic Jews (present-day Jewish believers in Jesus/*Yeshua* as the Messiah, the Son of God and the only Savior of mankind) often face for celebrating

holidays unique to the Jewish culture. But we need to discern between the propriety of a Messianic Jewish believer's celebration of timeless events within the framework of their *culture* and the proposition that "this practice is a regressive dependence upon the Law rather than grace." Such criticism is as meaningless as assailing an American Christian for celebrating the Fourth of July or Thanksgiving.

Only for Starters

These issues only open a subject that calls the whole church to awareness and sensitivity if a present, prophetically pregnant moment is to birth its possibilities. Otherwise, we may unwittingly mirror the very thing done by many believing Jews in New Testament times. Though born again themselves, they rejected Gentiles who had received Jesus as the Messiah/Savior unless they practiced *Jewish* traditions! (See Galatians 1-2; Romans 1-4.) But that "renewal" was sustained as Jerusalem's church leaders (all of them Jewish!) took discerning action, and God's Word triumphed over human misunderstanding. (See Acts 11:1-18; 15:1-32.)

May the same Holy Spirit of renewal help us in the same way today. The times in which we are invite it. The Holy Spirit of truth requires it, and it is rooted in the belief that the revelation of God's Word relates an End-Times spiritual awakening among the Jews to a global move of the Holy Spirit in reviving, life-giving power. (See Romans 11:12, 15, 25; Luke 21:24, 28–33.)

Jack Hayford, "Reaching His Chosen People," *Ministries Today* (March/April 2001): 20–21.

Sharpening Your Leading Edge

If a leader's character can be found strong enough, his mind honest enough and his heart soft enough—the course of maturing leadership will open into the realm of statesmanship, depending upon the arena of God's assigned purpose for him or her. As such, a statesman is a leader who can see beyond his own environment, agenda and convictions and reach to others who may differ from him or even reject his values, and still be a bridge builder and a peacemaker. A statesman is not a compromiser of his own convictions, but a person of understanding toward those whose convictions are different.

I believe *any* leader—business or otherwise—who is a believer needs to think through such matters as follow in this pair of articles. In today's church there is a great need for an increase in leaders (lay and clergy alike) who will allow themselves to become statesmen. This is not a role one invites for himself, but if it evolves, it is a place of service that others recognize and acknowledge. To do so requires a refusal of the vain presumption that any of us "completely understand" anything! Understanding only comes with the humble acknowledgment that God is God alone, and only He understands completely.

Notwithstanding the limited scope of the immediate subject of these articles and the brevity of their remarks, I offer these thoughts in their original form in the hope they may stimulate the consideration of that stance and attitude, which, to my view, cultivate *grace* in the soul, *breadth* in the vision and *unity* in the body of Christ. I do not expect agreement with my conclusions. I would long for agreeableness with my quest for a mutual reaching-to-touch-in-peace throughout the evangelical community. It has to be a superior stance to the judgmentalism, suspicion, blackballing and carping that is always evident where self-righteousness and separatism survive.

For More...

Reading of revivals past, in reports revisionists have not had a chance to flavor to their tastes, inevitably reveals the fact that God's visitations are never "neat." It is not that God is sloppy; it is that we are—like small children—learning to eat and drink the fresh bread and new wine of revival, and it ends up as much around us as within us.

Search out such writings as those of Finney, of Moody, of the Wesleys, of the early Nazarenes, Pentecostals and other "holiness" seekers.

Consider *Surprised by the Power of the Spirit* by Jack Deere for a blend of theology and experience in discussing God at work in power today.[5]

Also, read *Hosting the Holy Spirit*, edited by Che Ahn—a collection of testimonies from people touched by the Toronto visitation and other revivals.[6]

[chapter 6] Our Stance Before Almightiness

NOT long ago, the "Toronto Blessing" seemed to be on every leader's tongue. Because of mixed reviews, I asked church leaders, "What have you found yourself saying about the reports of renewal and unusual phenomena at the Toronto Airport Vineyard church?"

I don't feel constrained to understand everything that turns up in the name of God. It doesn't bother me to say, "Beats me!" when someone lays an imponderable on me.

But I intend to express some things that may assist some who are trying, as I am, to strike a sensitive and scriptural stance before the splendor of a "God thing." I say "God thing" because whatever anyone thinks about the events at the Toronto Vineyard, there seems to be evidence of a work of God—however attended it may be with signs of human frailty or imperfection.

I'm reminded of a patriarch in my past who quoted Genesis 1:1: "In the beginning, GOD!" He would intone the last word with such force and finality that you were left with a sense of awe, finiteness, humility and dependency. That emphatic "GOD!" provided for some of my earliest lessons in standing silent before the Almighty. His actions may bewilder or delight me, but His wisdom, "Be still and know that I am God," was etched into my soul.

I realize that better minds than mine have judged both the Toronto events and its overflow elsewhere, judged it to be not only unworthy of Christian conduct but also quite removed from the majesty of God. But even though those minds may be better, I'm not sure they are necessarily wiser in this case.

Jesus Glorified

Whatever peculiarities of this visitation may puzzle us, one inescapable fact remains: Jesus Christ is being glorified. Something about that fact sounds like the Holy Spirit to me.

I have no agenda in making these observations. I've not been to Toronto, though I've conversed with trusted, no-nonsense brethren who have.

I have nothing to sell and no one to defend because I haven't met any of the primary leaders at the center of this phenomenon. But I do have a pastoral concern—along with a personal, "acquired disposition" that prompts my writing this. My pastoral concern is toward good pastors and other church leaders whose reaction to the so-called Toronto Blessing is *fearful*. I'm referencing an almost frenetic anxiety that I've noticed among a few good leaders who have been struck by desperation of sorts.

Some appear to feel guilt—a suspicion they may be "out of it" because Toronto-style signs aren't appearing at their church. They hop a jet for Canada, driven less by spiritual hunger than by fear they will somehow earn divine disapproval if they don't go. My heart goes out to dear people who fear that God won't visit them if they don't visit Toronto.

On the other hand, any of us are liable to smugness in our passivity. I've had to ask myself, *Is the reason I haven't visited because I feel it's beneath me?* (Or worse—because I'd end up on my back, laughing uncontrollably?) But with an open heart to the Holy Spirit, I think I can answer, "I haven't made the flight because I'm confident of God's bigness."

I'm convinced that it's impossible to confine His creative, renewing, reviving works to one place or to one set of manifestations. And I'm certain, wherever our geographical

REFUSING TO BE BLUNTED—TEMPERING MY PERCEPTUAL "EDGE"

location may be, that "He satisfies the longing soul, and fills the hungry soul with goodness" (Ps. 107:9). In other words, if you truly want Him, He'll show up wherever you are.

As sure as I am that God will answer the heart of anyone who passionately seeks Him, I'm also certain of another fact. Even though "He has filled the hungry with good things," yet "the rich He has sent away empty" (Luke 1:53).

That's what reinforces my "acquired disposition"—my awe of God requires me to give Him space in the face of the unusual. I realize some may interpret my slowness to pass judgment as negligent or cowardly. But the ways I have experienced God in my past cause me to allow for His creativity to exceed my wishes, my systems or my comfort zone.

Why? In short because the Lord still only lavishes His grace and glory on those who admit they're poor. The "poor in spirit" are recipients of the kingdom (Matt. 5:3). They are the ones willing to admit, "I don't have it all, and I can't get what I need by my own wisdom or strength."

Such "poverty" is something I dare never outgrow. The minute I believe that the deep riches I've come to know in Christ are meant to secure me from my continuous need for a teachable heart and a childlike, seeking soul, then I am being duped by false definitions of maturity, discernment or knowledge.

Look at the Fruit

Believe me, dear friend, as baffling and undesirable to most human tastes as the phenomena accompanying the Toronto Blessing may be, the fact is that multitudes have been stirred to new devotion to Jesus or retrieved from unnecessary pain or bondage.

Is the flesh present in this blessing? Surely! But show me a place where blessing has ever come and been handled with absolute human perfection.

The very proposition that flesh can stand before the glory of God and maintain its dignity and composure is smug in its very conception. How can any of us suggest that almightiness could move among us and we still be able to entertain it with cool aplomb?

What's the source? Could the source of unusual phenomena be the inability of frail humanity to contain the mightiness of divine breakthrough? Whatever manifestations should be discounted because of spiritual thrill-seeking or power-ofsuggestion responses by some, I think we're wise to give almighty God space and recognize man's small place.

This requires allowing the full reign of the Spirit's power to undercut our style-consciousness and desire for respectability. I don't say this because I believe God is laying people low with laughter and producing barking sounds as an intentional act of humiliation. But I do believe that unperceived resistance is being cut through by a patient Father who doesn't mind where the chips fall. That human beings so encountered by God's almightiness don't look all that strong, neat or wise probably matters little to Him. And that the apparent "antics" annoy some or produce accusations of fanaticism by others is probably unavoidable.

Revival critics are always present in every age. Their voices argue for caution and claim biblical sanity. But God's ways do not always answer to the humanly "sane." While neither goofy nor giddy, God seems to readily do things that confound human intellect. And that's why long ago I decided to live in the light of Gamaliel's "wait and see" attitude. I believe Isaiah's recorded "word from heaven" about God's ways and thoughts being a lot higher than mine.

So if you see a bush blaze without being burned or tongues

of fire fill a room while people there begin to speak strange languages, it might be wise *not* to stance yourself to criticize, however bewildered. A far more biblical stance before such almightiness is twofold—take off your shoes, and if you open to the God who is present and speaking, you might end up facing charges of drunkenness.

Jack Hayford, "Our Stance Before Almightiness," *Ministries Today* (May/June 1995): 24–25.

[chapter 7] The Bugaboo and the Blessing

TALK of the Toronto Blessing doesn't seem to go away. By now you've probably heard the news about the Toronto Airport Vineyard's dismissal from the Association of Vineyard Churches. The goal, it seems, is to allow the two of them to determine their future without reliance on the other. Yet the separation inevitably brings up questions, and my mailbox and phone pad have displayed considerable inquiry. "Jack, where do you stand on this?" many people have asked. Whether or not you are one who has wrestled with Toronto Blessing questions, I think there are some guiding principles from the Word that may be of interest.

First, in an earlier article, I described how when faced with happenings such as Toronto I generally take Gamaliel's stand (Acts 5:33–39). I believe the whole body of Christ would be better served if we all avoided the urging of those who ask us to nitpick issues of difference in the church. However, without taking sides on the decision to dismiss the Toronto church from the Vineyard fellowship, I think we who lead must face the pastoral issue the action raises. What responsibility do we have not only to feed and lead the flock, but also to administrate biblical authority—in this case by "governing" meetings where manifestations of the Holy Spirit are evident?

The "Quench Not" Bugaboo

Perhaps no biblical prohibition should cause more trepidation to spiritual leaders than "quench not the Spirit" (1 Thess. 5:19, KJV). This causes a dilemma for leaders who value the moving of the Spirit. What degree of responsibility should be taken to maintain order in a given setting, and how can this be done without violating the Holy Spirit's freedom to work?

Apprehension about quenching the Spirit frequently becomes a bugaboo of sorts—a kind of haunting fear that prompts some pastors to forfeit an appropriate exercise of spiritual government in meetings they lead. Often the ensuing disorder distorts an understanding of what God is really doing. And worse, the entire ungoverned environment gives place to dismayed or critical judgments that might not have come if the governing responsibility of pastoral care had been more wisely carried out. The command that we not *quench* (*shennumi* in Greek) does not employ a word that denotes a hands-off posture—the verb is related to handling fire. It describes action that extinguishes a blaze, not efforts to keep the blaze under reasonable control.

Administrating the Blaze

The beneficial power of fire to ignite, warm, release energy or destroy things that are undesirable is maximized when it's "governed." Without any restraints, however, the destructive power of fire is notorious. Not long ago, a group of forest service workers set a controlled fire in our area to burn off areas of potential threat to our community. It was fascinating to watch how they "administrated" the fire. Their attentive, restraining influence assured that this "blessing" didn't become caught by a gust of wind that caused it to exceed the boundaries of intended good. This illustrates a valid biblical paradigm. It is what Paul was seeking to help the Corinthian leadership understand and apply when he exhorted them about the proper operation of spiritual manifestations in their meetings.

In Corinth, the blessing that needed governing was speaking in tongues. Today the same principles can well be applied to other "signs."

Drawing that analogy, we can note five things from 1 Corinthians 14 about a pastor's responsibility to teach and administrate amid the supernatural works of God:

1. **It is a valid objective to avoid, as much as possible, "appearing crazy" (v. 23).**

While mockers will always deride the works of God, onlookers generally should be able to see that there are at least some behavioral guidelines. This doesn't mean we attempt to reduce the miraculous to a set of empirical categories. It does mean, however, that as a teacher of the Word of God I am charged with explaining and interpreting the work of the Holy Spirit as best I can. Although holy happenings may bring charges of "drunkenness" (Acts

2:13), my role isn't to revel in the accusation—it's to give a reasoned response (Acts 2:14–16).

2. **Governing sometimes requires us to limit or disallow supernatural operations that are excessive or untimely (vv. 28–31).**

The Bible is clear that wisdom often means applying restraints—even when some of what is disallowed would have been spiritually valid. The text does not say additional manifestations of "tongues" would not be of the Holy Spirit. Instead, the reason for some restraint seems clear: The novelty of some supernatural expressions has a way of eventually creating an atmosphere of sensationalism. Ungoverned, the meaning and message in the Spirit's work can too easily become subordinated to the dramatic manifestation itself. Even in the atmosphere of the Holy Spirit's working it seems that "too much candy can ruin your teeth."

3. **Those governing need to realize that a person experiencing supernatural manifestations of the Holy Spirit usually has the ability to maintain a certain degree of self-control (v. 32).**

A Spirit-filled person is not a Spirit-seized person. Under the auspices of this text, though, some may actually quench the Spirit's work because they are uncomfortable with anything supernatural. Any fire carries with it the possibility of a temporary loss of control. Yet I want to remain more willing to risk an outbreak from gusty winds than to risk the possibility of having no fire at all.

4. **Governing is the responsibility of people who are truly spiritual (v. 37).**

As in Paul's day, there are always those who purport a superior spirituality because they refuse to accept any restraints amid the supernatural. Paul's guidelines to the Corinthian church can give us confidence that it's OK to maintain order when our openness to the Spirit has brought events that seem on the verge of being out of control. The proper balance is difficult to define with precision. I've been inclined to adopt the perspective I once heard quoted from John Wesley: "I'd rather try to tame a wild horse than resurrect a dead one!"

5. **No leader is ever authorized to govern in such a way that the supernatural operations of the Spirit are totally suppressed (vv. 39–40).**

We are told to see that everything is done "decently" (the Greek means "gracious and charming in character") and "in order" (which means appropriate priorities are maintained and things occur in a sensible sequence). God never authorizes confusion. He expects us to govern even things that may bewilder us.

To govern biblically means using our authority to serve a situation, not dominate it; to release its possibilities, not restrict its potential. Pastors with a passion for the supernatural—and to this I plead guilty—face a dual challenge:

- **To be so cautious as to utterly disallow the "fire and wind" is to assure an eventual chilled and stale atmosphere, however orderly.**

- **But to let things "flap in the wind" without restraint is to give place to an eventual whirlwind of confusion (Hos. 8:7).**

I salute any pastor or leader who is: 1) committed to the supernatural manifestations of the Spirit; 2) responsible to exercise pastoral government amid such manifestations; and 3) continually laboring to ground the flock in a solid rootedness in the unchanging truth of God's written Word. People led and fed in that way will never be blown about by the wind or burned out by the fire. Instead, those Spirit-generated forces will only refresh and ignite their potential.

Jack Hayford, "The Bugaboo and the Blessing," *Ministries Today* (March/April 1996): 24–25.

Section 2

Letting "Iron Sharpen Iron"

Discipling the Leader's Mindset

It is one thing to face issues and demands; it is another to choose new realms of development in life, thought and leadership. The ongoing renewal of the human mind is a prerequisite to experiencing the Creator's unfolding purpose for each person (Rom. 12:1-2). Essentially, that renewal is not an intellectual exercise—it is born of a mindset that accepts a dual discipline:

1. To respect and persistently advance in the time-proven basics that give foundation and substance to life

2. To reflect and insistently accept the present-season realities of transition occurring—and to connect the transitional with the foundational

These six articles are intended to give, through contact with each one, an already keen mind something to be further sharpened by—from the timeless to the timely principles and processes of God's Word and way.

Sharpening Your Leading Edge

This article targets the provision of yet another "list"—this being a summary of those disciplines that I, first of all, must come to terms with as a leader. The object is not to induce guilt over neglected areas, but to "sharpen iron" with the substance of those proven features of discipleship that grow depth, breadth and height in a believer's life. The gifted leader's capacity to achieve things "on the fly" can easily breed a neglect of basic discipleship and the character development the disciplines shape in us. That simple observation is enough to challenge the issue. The true leader's "edge" is found in pursuing the <u>disciplined life</u>—it's <u>the only safe atmosphere</u> in which to exercise the benefits of <u>a gifted life</u>.

For More...

Investigate two contemporary classics on Christian discipline: *The Spirit of the Disciplines* by Dallas Willard and *Celebration of Discipline* by Richard Foster.[7]

And may I suggest you also consider *Living the Spirit-Formed Life,* which I wrote to provide practical, nonmystical steppingstones to applying the Christian disciplines to life.[8] This three-hundred-page volume develops the ten disciplines outlined in this article. It has both video and/or audio resources, available from Living Way Ministries, for personal, classroom, small group or congregational use.

[chapter 8]

The "Happy" in the Disciplines

"GRANDPA," the voice spoke cautiously. I started—turning with surprise, just that moment noticing movement from the corner of my eye.

"Oh, Jack!" I inhaled deeply—smiling. "You kinda' scared me. I didn't hear you come up the stairs." The twelve-year-old seemed embarrassed, surprising me as I was engrossed in my study, so I reached over, patted his shoulder and said, "How's everything goin'?"

"OK," he returned, still somewhat uneasy, then he added, "I wanted to tell you about something the Lord showed me the other day."

I nodded toward a chair, signaling, "Pull it up over here by me. I'd like to hear about it." It was nice to have him in town with his sister, mom and dad (our oldest son) visiting from Wisconsin. It was two days after Thanksgiving, and as I pushed my chair back from the desk to give him my full attention, I didn't know I was about to gain yet another reason for being thankful. I invited him to continue. "What was it the Lord showed you?"

His eyes were bright with excitement, and he started to rush his words as though needing to hurry (still, I suppose, feeling awkward for having surprised me as he had). "Take your time, Jack (he's named after me!), I really want to hear this." He relaxed a little more in his chair, and then began again.

"Well, the other day I got to thinking about something I read in my devotions. It's in Proverbs 12:1, where it says 'Whoever loves discipline loves knowledge, but he who hates correction is stupid'" (NIV). He quoted the verse, then paused. I nodded approvingly, and he went on. "I was thinking, *Why would anyone want to be **disciplined!?*** You know what I mean, Grandpa? Like, who would ever LOVE to be punished, or even spanked?" He could see I understood his point.

"Then it's like, all of a sudden, something happened in my heart. I realized that if discipline keeps you from doing dumb things—you know, stuff that's really going to wreck your life, messing you up so all kinds of bad stuff happens— then discipline is really a good thing. And then, I felt like I could understand. It made me really want to learn to *love discipline."* He stopped to see if I was following...accepting what he was saying. But I was far more than "accepting"—I was on the edge of tears.

"Jack, that is absolutely great!" He read my smile for its intended message—more than mere approval—and my brief handclasp on his knee was more than a warm gesture. I wanted him to know his insight was not only *right,* but it was deep—that it reveals a heart that is touching a pivotal issue for any of us who would truly hope to *know God.* I said as much. As I did, it was a great "happy" for my own soul, and our conversation continued as I urged him to elaborate more of how this "moment" in his own soul had happened, more about what he felt it meant to him.

Knowing he not only loves his Grandpa, but also that he has a special feeling for the fact he carries my name, I wanted to be sure he sensed my affirmation was more than simply a courtesy. For the reality is that child-brinking-teen-years has struck the chord that produces the prospect for anyone or everyone discovering and living a life of harmony—tuned to God's Word, then willing to learn His ways, whatever it takes!

All Disciplines Are Blessings

My heart rejoiced! It was not only over hearing my grandson

relate the Holy Spirit-ignited insight given to his heart, but even more in seeing his maturing desire to *respond* to that truth—to commit to its meaning for his daily life. My heart leaped in me as he shared it, because I don't know of *anything* more important to my whole life in Christ than having early learned two things:

1. **Always invite and welcome the Lord's correction and instruction, and refuse to argue your own "righteousness."**

2. **Continually seek and pursue patterns of basic Christian disciplines, even when it seems you may never perfect any of them!**

Life's disciplines are not punishments—the punishments are the friction that "burns our hide" when we move outside the life-flow of God's best ways for living!

All discipline—from the *principles* to the *corrections* when we violate the basics in the principles—is a blessing. To learn, understand and grow in the disciplines of life is to move in the direction of life's fullest fruitfulness, fulfillment and joy!

Thinking About the Principles

Young Jack, my grandson, "got the picture." He recognized that at the root of it all, disciplines are benefits—instruction more than punishment. The keys to learning that instruction are well established in God's Word and have been set forth for God's people in practical principles that we can learn to live in—*joyfully!*

That's why my teaching calendar begins each year with a focus on basic principles of growth through discipline. In fact, a recent year began with two Wednesday evenings (before a near full house) outlining the Word's wisdom, ways and joys in the discovering of ten basic disciplines of New Testament living. "The Ten Disciplines of the Disciple" focused on the importance of each and on a pathway of application. I believe wise leaders will not only pursue discipline in their own lives, but will also answer the call to cultivate the same *grace* (not laws) in others. To help point the way, let me provide a grid of the fundamental disciplines with a summary of the principle behind each point of discipleship. As you use it, consider measuring your present response, and then set your course—to teach and to live—to *deepen* in the power of the disciplined life. I hope it proves a helpful "launching pad" toward putting believers "into orbit" around the Sun of Righteousness—Jesus Himself. He's the One who calls us *to* discipleship. And He's the One who will help us *make* disciples!

Ten Disciplines of the Disciple

Discipline #1: Committing to hear God's voice

My sheep hear My voice, and I know them, and they follow Me.

—John 10:27

Principle: To read and study God's Word is to lay the foundation for all understanding and growth. However, the Bible is a living Word that has not been given to us solely for information, analysis and education. God wants to speak to each one of His children, to teach and correct, to lead and direct, to keep and protect. For this to take place vitally and ongoingly, the believer needs to learn to hear the "word" within the Word—to receive the prophetic intent of the Holy Spirit breathing truth into our hearts in order to transform our lives.

Discipline #2: Living in the power of water baptism

Thus it is fitting for us to fulfill all righteousness.

—Matthew 3:15

Principle: Jesus' command to all who receive His life-gift of salvation is that they be baptized in water—a call to experience a dynamic, not merely to observe a duty. To obey is a point of entrance into a river-like pathway of submission to the lordship of Christ, committing to pursue discipleship as one "dead unto sin but alive to God" through the power of the Holy Spirit.

Discipline #3: Receiving the resources of the Lord's Table

Take, eat; this is My body...Drink...all of you.

—MATTHEW 26:26–27

Principle: The observance of the Lord's Table is a practice that frames the centerpiece of Christian faith—the Cross—and a priority that focuses on the central Person of our worship, Jesus our Savior. To participate with understanding is to transcend mere tradition and to open to the present dynamic the Holy Spirit will bring where the living Word and living worship converge to release the power of Christ's presence at His Table.

Discipline #4: Continuing in the spirit of forgiveness

I forgave you...Should you not also have had compassion...?

—MATTHEW 18:32–33

Principle: The forgiveness of sin given freely to us in Christ through His atoning death and justifying work opens a foun-tainhead of grace that flows to us without measure. That same measure of graciousness is a summons to every believer, saying, "Freely you have received, freely give"—a call that cannot remain unanswered except at the expense of blockage, bondage and withering of soul.

Discipline #5: Feeding on the Word of God

Man shall not live by bread alone, but by every word that proceeds from the mouth of God.

—MATTHEW 4:4

Principle: Persistence on a daily pathway, progressing through the Bible, though beset by distraction and schedule irregularity, is not only essential—it can be joyous! God's Word is the ever-available supernatural source for faith, strength, wisdom, growth and freedom in Christ, and there is no substitute for its power to nurture, counsel and sustain.

Discipline #6: Maintaining integrity of heart

Blessed are the pure in heart, for they shall see God.

—MATTHEW 5:8

Principle: Contrary to the ideas of Western intellectualism, God is not known via the mind but via the heart. Our intelligence may deduce things about Him, and our minds study realities revealed by Him, but God is ultimately known in Person and in intimacy by those who seek Him with all their hearts. Once He is met and known, advancement on the path to maturity and personal effectiveness is realized in the fullest way only as a discipline of purity and totality of heart-yieldedness and vulnerability to the Holy Spirit is maintained in humility and childlikeness.

Discipline #7: Abiding in the fullness of the Holy Spirit

He who believes in Me, as the Scripture has said, out of his heart will flow rivers of living water.

—JOHN 7:38

Principle: Nothing in the believer's life is more essential to his or her becoming a daily, fully empowered replication and representative of Jesus Christ than being and keeping filled with the Holy Spirit. From Pentecost until our Lord's return, the church's commission is to receive "power from on high," "do business till I come," "go into all the world" and to experience "the Lord working with them and confirming the word through the accompanying signs" (Luke 24:49; 19:13; Mark 16:15–20). The full mandate is only possible through being baptized in the Holy Spirit (Acts 1:5-8; 2:1-4) and continually being freshly filled with His love and power (Rom. 5:6; Acts 4:8; 7:55; 13:52; Eph. 5:18-20).

Discipline # 8: Living a life of submission

> If anyone desires to come after Me, let him deny himself, and take up his cross, and follow Me.
>
> —MATTHEW 16:24

Principle: As disciples of Jesus, we have been called to the One, "who, being in very nature God, did not consider equality with God something to be grasped, but…taking the very nature of a servant…he humbled himself and became obedient to…even death on a cross" (Phil. 2:6-8, NIV). The pathway of biblical surrender is not only to yield to Christ as Lord, but also to follow Him as the Servant who "did not come to be served, but to serve, and to give His life a ransom for many" (Matt. 20:28).

Discipline #9: The practice of solitude

> In the morning, having risen a long while before daylight, He went out and departed to a solitary place; and there He prayed.
>
> —MARK 1:35

Principle: The disciple must learn the wisdom and the habit

of regularly experiencing both the private, personal presence of God and the benefit of personal time and space away from life's daily demands. Without it, life and service will become a blur, producing discouragement, distraction or defeat. With it, life is regularly being recharged with energy and spiritual dynamic.

Discipline #10: Pursuing the life of a worshiper

The hour is coming...when the true worshipers will worship the Father in spirit and truth; for the Father is seeking such to worship Him.

—JOHN 4:23

Principle: Worship is the ultimate priority of every believer, not only because God is worthy of our worship, but because it is His designed means to arrange His entry into our personal world as well as those circumstances where His sovereign workings have placed us. Worship is the capstone to the ten primary disciplines because it opens the doorway to God's superintendency and supernatural presence and power as the governing influence and the purifying element in all life issues. Worship is also the pathway into prayer—the all-encompassing discipline—and is prayer's essential point of entry to the Father and of faith in His almightiness.

Prayer: The Overarching Discipline

It is fully intentional that *prayer* is not listed in the ten basic disciplines. This is certainly not because it is optional or unimportant, but because it is so central to the actuation of *all* disciplines and the pursuit of *all* of a disciple's life that it would seem misleading to place it within the list.

Prayer in all its forms spreads out to overarch the structures of the disciplines. It is both the roof and the skylight, just as the Word of God provides the footings and the foundation. But it is different from the reading and study of God's Word in the scope of the variety of exercises available and the dimensions of depth that may be realized. Because prayer moves beyond the comprehensible at times, it opens that which is "above all that we ask or think" (Eph. 3:20).

Worship, exaltation, adoration, thanksgiving and praise join with confession, repentance, petition, supplication, intercession and warfare—together and intertwining. Prayer in its manifold expressions forms an indescribable spectrum of wonder in our approach to, seeking of, growing in, asking of and knowing God.

Ultimately, intimacy in *knowing God through prayer*

transcends all the possibilities of insight in *discovering God through His Word.* This in no wise minimizes the essential wisdom of reading, studying and growing in the Word of truth. It is simply an honest and needed acknowledgment—the deepest knowledge of God is never acquired through the human mind but by the human spirit. Thus, prayer becomes the school where all we would know, learn, live and apply of the Lord and His ways is initiated in our *life* to become incarnated in our *living.*

Take inventory. Begin it *thoughtfully* in God's presence, and grow in it *prayerfully* by His Spirit's power. "He who has begun a good work in you will complete it until the day of Jesus Christ" (Phil. 1:6).

———————————————

Original article for this book

Sharpening Your Leading Edge

The phenomenal dimensions of the "awakening" of millions of Christian men to their own role as servant-leaders puts a pointed question to all church leaders: "Am I answering to this feature of my call as a leader?" In the following two articles, I describe the way I was drawn into a practical, functional and fruitful ministry to the men in my congregation. Within the rise of that productive and powerful development, I came to discover that certain thought patterns—both in my mind and in theirs—were essential if we were to find durability to the movement of God's Spirit among men. These are those introductory means we employed and one of the primary concepts that has sustained a "movement" in our midst for nearly thirty years.

For More...

Today, every Christian bookstore offers a plethora of material on men—an evidence of the "awakening" to which I refer. PromiseKeepers continues to make a great impact—now, primarily, of cultivating resources for local church leadership usage and also in their new focus on "Passage"—the shaping of boys into godly men. (Dads and youth pastors deserve a "heads up" on this development.)

In *Pastors of Promise* I develop a complete resource for evolving both a biblical mindset and a practical program for a ministry to men at the local level.[9]

At www.jackhayford.com you can also find interactive studies for men, built on my six books for men themed The Power to Become series.[10]

Finally, because of my many years of speaking to men concerning all points of masculine development as a man, husband, citizen, employer, employee and servant of Jesus Christ, a large selection of audiocassette studies are available. A catalog is available at Living Way's website at www.livingway.com.

[chapter 9]

Shaping Men—
Shaping the Church

IT was cold—biting, below-zero, Illinois-in-February cold—as I walked down the small country path in the early morning through foot-deep snow.

I trudged along—earmuffs, scarf, heavy cap, jacket, boots and all—watching the sun rise over the southeast, a purplish-orange ball cresting over snow-laden trees. As bitter as the cold was, it was a delightful, "winter wonderland" moment.

Even though frozen ice crystals formed as my breath touched the air, the morning was sheer magnificence. It was one of those precious, nonstressed moments, encompassed by God's awesome creation—the kind of moment I'd want to remember on a July day while driving the Los Angeles freeways during rush hour.

I was in the Midwest to fulfill a speaking engagement, and I have to admit I was enjoying the winter scene so thoroughly for one basic reason: I had flown in to speak, and I could fly right out when I was finished. Winter on demand—without pain!

I continued walking, every step a crunch under my feet. I had no idea it was in this setting that God was about to meet me. I was entirely unprepared for what would become one of the most important assignments ever impressed upon my heart concerning how I was to lead as a pastor and how I myself was to live in the ensuing years.

Just a year before, our small congregation had experienced a dramatic visitation of God's grace. In that twelve-month period, we'd quadrupled—grown from one hundred people to just over four hundred.

Of course, I didn't have the slightest dream that our church would take on the mega proportions it eventually has—now serving eight to ten thousand people in public services each week. The four hundred was "plenty of miracle" for me!

So that morning, as my feet crunched the frozen country pathway, my heart was full. I'd seen a year of incredible blessing. And now, here I was, surrounded by the beauty of God's winter creation.

It was then the words came: "I want you to begin to gather

men and train them. As you do, I will raise up strong leadership for the future of this church."

Though I didn't understand all the implications at that moment, I did sense God's desire to build men—strong men, strong single guys, strong husbands, strong fathers who knew who they were in Christ.

Our Starting Place

About six weeks later I began monthly men's meetings at The Church On The Way. We called them "Men's Growth Seminars." For the first meeting, I sent a note with a direct invitation to thirty-five men and also put a general announcement in the church bulletin.

Eighteen came. So we made a circle of chairs—a simple, close-together arrangement. We had a time of worship, and then I opened my heart to them about God's "word" to me. And that's how it started.

Looking back, I can report that what happened that winter morning—now more than twenty years ago—affected not only my own life, but drastically (and very beautifully) the whole of the congregation I serve. God's assignment that day made an impact so great it still resonates through and orchestrates my thoughts, pastoral values and ministry.

Over the years there have been multiplied thousands who have been influenced. The direct result is that as our church has grown, there have been stable underpinnings, not only through vital, Christ-exalting worship and Word-centered preaching, but also through the roles filled by a cadre of committed, growing, sensible, submitted, godly men.

Why should—and how could—such a strategy make so much difference?

God's Redemptive Sequence

Let me make a head-on statement at the risk of generating sparks. In our sometimes militantly feminist society, it's more than likely that some people won't listen no matter how carefully I explain. But to begin, let me say this: In most of His workings, God starts with men.

I am in no way suggesting that men are superior to women. Neither am I hinting at any rejection or reduction of the value of women in God's kingdom purposes.

But this fundamental understanding starts with a simple fact in Scripture—the sequence in creation: "Adam was formed first" (1 Tim. 2:13). It's this sequence that God has chosen to preserve in His redemptive "order" of dealing with humankind.

There's a functional purpose to that order. It isn't that by making man first, God prefers him. It is that having made man first in the initial Creation, He has chosen to deal with man first in His quest to recover what the Fall has brought about.

Just as God, in Creation, started with man (in order to later form woman from his side and thereby demonstrate the union and heart-commitment He intended the couple to have), so in Redemption He begins with men to demonstrate something. That "something" is the target of our men's ministries—to recover something of the understanding we men have lost about our responsibilities under God.

God is unapologetic about this plan He has of "starting things" with men. It's threaded through His Word. Consider that:

[■] The human race began with a man—Adam.

[■] The vision of faith's promise—how to walk a pathway of faith with God—began with a man—Abraham.

- [■] The Jewish people began with a man—Jacob—to whom God reached out and called, saying, "I will make of you a great nation."

- [■] Israel's deliverance from Egypt—which is a grand picture of God's whole deliverance program for all mankind through the blood of the Lamb—came under the leadership of a man—Moses.

- [■] Israel's possession of Canaan came under the leadership of a man—Joshua—who led the people of God into their inheritance. Joshua became the biblical type of Jesus, who, as our Leader, brings us into the possession of our God-promised destinies.

- [■] The precursor of Messiah, the royal prototype of the One who would become humanity's King, was a man—David.

- [■] And finally, when God became flesh to rescue all mankind, He came as a man—in the form of His Son, Jesus Christ, the ultimate man, the second Adam, the Son of God.

In underscoring these facts, I would not, nor could I, dismiss the worth or preciousness of womanhood. Nothing about God's order reduces the marvelous role of the woman nor suggests a heavenly rejection of her significance.

But historically and redemptively, God has most commonly

led the way—releasing His purposes in the interest of all humanity—through the leadership of men. Men are God's "starting place."

Developing Spiritual Manhood

If a church is deficient in spiritual vitality, you can usually find the root by asking, "What place is being given to the development of men?" It's generally true that when God breaks through in a church, it's because He's making a breakthrough with men—to shape the men...to shape the church.

That does not minimize women (see the next chapter). It does confront a reality—historically women seem more spiritually responsive than men. That responsiveness is beautiful. But there's a need to come full circle in a holy breakthrough in men.

I believe that's the reason the Lord dealt with me that winter day in Illinois. When men are strong in the ways of the Lord, the expansion of the kingdom of God not only advances—it accelerates. Spiritual manhood affects everything!

Manhood on God's terms is foundational to:

1. *A new mindset for single men.* This creates a new cultural context with non-self-centered men who don't

exploit women and who understand their own life purpose and thereby serve God effectively.

2. *Fullest husbandhood.* Godly manhood is the beginning of a marriage that works, because the man loves his wife as Christ loved the church and gave Himself up for it.

3. *Fullest fatherhood.* Well-adjusted children are those who have a happy, loved mom as well as a dad who is diligent to fulfill his role in the family unit.

4. *Godly business relationships.* True manhood uniquely touches the business world. Men become successful when they know who they are as men in Christ. They succeed not by reason of falsely competitive machismo or manipulative scheming, but by God's grace working His highest creative purposes for each one.

5. *Vital churches.* Godly manhood releases life in the local church as the relevance of Christ is manifested and as the notions that "spirituality is unmanly" and "Christians are wimps" are buried—permanently!

If manhood is diminished, perverted, unbalanced, misunderstood, impotent or destructive—anything less than accurately reflective of the image of Christ—then the church and the world take a loss at every level.

Marriages tend to become weak or dissolve. Children tend

to be unstable and deficient. Businesses lose out. The church is stultified.

In short, men lead the way, whether for good or no good.

In contrast, understanding God's sequential order concerning men in leadership roles will bring God's release to everyone—men and women. True biblical teaching will bring a holy freedom that actually elevates womanhood.

Iron Sharpening Iron

Just as God's starting point is with men, a man's starting place is to align his relationships with God's ways.

There are three primary areas of relationship that are critical in shaping men. The first is with God. The second is with his wife, if he's married. The third is with other men.

This latter area is perhaps the least discussed in church circles. Yet the Bible clearly shows that a man who would become the maximum person God intends him to be must discover the power and blessing of partnership with other men.

Jesus demonstrated this need for partnering in man-to-man relationships. He gathered a dozen men together, shaping them to make them shapers of the whole world—and their impact has continued right to this present day.

Contrary to popular belief, men aren't born. Children are born—men are formed. The Bible says men help form one another: "As iron sharpens iron, so a man sharpens...his friend" (Prov. 27:17).

Men are carved, designed and shaped into true manhood. And at the core of that process is the crucial component—man-to-man relationships, one of God's chief scalpels.

Being conformed to the image of Jesus can't be done "Lone Ranger" style. Prioritizing the cultivation of such relationships according to God's created order is an essential, practical biblical principle, in line with His blueprint for full manhood.

Friendships not only reflect the man, but they can make him what he is. They decide his depth, his qualities, his skills and his destiny. As Scripture says, "He who walks with wise men will be wise, but the companion of fools will be destroyed" (Prov. 13:20).

There's a profound shaping of men that happens when we come together and learn to grow together in Christ. John wrote these words: "If we walk in the light as He is in the light, we have fellowship with one another, and the blood of Jesus Christ His Son cleanses us from all sin" (1 John 1:7).

Notice that if we'll get together (true fellowship in Christ), there's something that will happen to us all—the blood of Jesus Christ will keep on cleansing us from all sin. That's the way the tense in the original Greek text puts it.

Progressing in fellowship brings progression in victory over sin's clutchings at a man's body, soul and spirit. As men walk in the light with other brothers, there is a progressive sense of what has already been positionally secured in Christ.

Of course, our past sin was totally covered, atoned for in Christ and forgiven completely when we came to Him. But present sin still finds occasions to tempt and try us.

That's why in walking with Jesus, I need also to walk with my brothers in Him—to "walk in the light" of a growing relationship of friendship, partnership and accountability.

As a result, through a loving and brotherly confronting of one another—not with ridicule but with honest-to-God, face-to-face realism—our trusting transparency ("in the light") advances the work of righteousness in each of us. Through

LETTING "IRON SHARPEN IRON"—DISCIPLING THE LEADER'S MINDSET

our "fellowship with one another" we can discover a special operation of the sanctifying blood of Christ.

We need each other! That's the reason for men's gatherings—large and small—among Christ's own.

Unfortunately, many men never allow themselves the possibility of that kind of fellowship. So often, a men's fellowship becomes only a superficial get-together—paint a building, mow a lawn, play on a team, even have a Bible study.

Those, of course, are all good things for men to do. But men's activities are not a substitute for men coming together and interfacing on a personal, spiritual dimension.

No Greater Passion

It has been decades now since God first spoke to me, "Gather the men and begin to teach them." Yet to this day nothing is a greater passion with me. As a pastor, I would even sacrifice Sunday morning preaching if I needed to in order to meet with the men of my church.

Thankfully, I don't have to make that choice. But my priorities are clear. I want to touch God's starting point for everything else He does: men.

Jack Hayford, "Developing Spiritual Manhood: The Key to Vitality in the Church," *Ministries Today* (September/October 1994): 34–42.

[chapter 10] Men First: But for Right Reasons

A few years ago, I was asked to cosign a statement on biblical manhood and womanhood prepared and signed by several dozen evangelical scholars and leaders. The document's constitution-like set of scriptural affirmations and denials aimed to answer the modern need for clarification of the roles of each gender in a society where the distinct place of each has become blurred.

I *almost* signed. In light of the clear, contemporary call of the Holy Spirit to awaken Christian men to their role as men, I so much wanted to add my name to such a needed statement!

But I ended up writing the brother who had invited my endorsement, "Sorry, I can't do it." As good as the work was, I believe it was only *almost* right.

The central weakness of the document, in my view, was a proposition stating that the Bible's placement of men as first, in terms of providing leadership, is based on a supposedly God-ordered preferential appointment of male over female at the time of Creation. In other words, the paper's position was not simply that man has been assigned a leadership role in God's order, but that he was *created* with it. When I read this, my mental brakes locked and I screeched to a stop.

My concern was more than academic. With the welcomed and widespread rise of attention coming to men's ministries throughout the body of Christ today, I rejoice in any call to biblical manhood. I say, "Amen!" Let's retool every man for it, with all the implications true biblical manhood holds for husbands and fathers in assuming their responsible role— and for every believing man in responding to the Master's call to devotion, discipleship and dutiful evangelism.

And let's assert that men are to lead—to step forth first—not as substitutes for women, but as servants who lead the way so that others realize God's fullest potential for them. Men are ordained to lead. But the fact that the Word of God calls men "first" should not be founded on a worn-out ecclesiastical dogma persisting today. This "firstness" and its way of service must be established on divine revelation—on the facts of Scripture, not on the chauvinistic disposition of church tradition.

God's Intent

Let me put it plainly: There is no way that male authority or leadership over women can be properly deduced from the Bible as being the original intent of God. The Bible does show man as being assigned a distinct initiating *responsibility* with reference to the woman, but he is not assigned a higher authority. The combined records of the Creation in Genesis 1–2 establish two facts about the first pair:

- They were given equal authority. (See Genesis 1:27–28.)

- The man was assigned distinct responsibility. He was the one responsible to relay, share and beget this mutuality of partnership with the woman, who, solely by reason of creative sequence, arrived later. (See Genesis 2:7–25.)

In short, before the Fall of man, the divine order for rule, for dominion, for leadership was entirely equal between the first man and woman. Theirs was untainted joint-rule over all the earth and the affairs assigned to them by the Creator. At Creation there was no submission of the woman to the man enjoined—only the submission of both to their Maker and to His divine order for the fulfilling of their destiny. (*Egalitarian* is the term often used by those who hold that men and women have equal roles, and this original order was exactly that. But please note: I am not arguing for the *egalitarianism* being demanded by evangelical feminists, as the following paragraphs will attest.)

A New Order

In contrast to the male/female partnership in dominion before the Fall of man, a new order was decreed by Father God after the Fall—an order that both assigns the man's role to lead and, at the same time, asserts that the woman will likely chafe under the new order. Genesis 3:16 not only introduces the woman to the fact that childbirth with travail will now be hers (something her pre-Fall condition might have averted), but another pre-Fall condition is altered by the words, "...your desire shall be for your husband."

This phrase has been subjected to many interpretations, but too seldom the correct one. The Hebrew verb *teshuquah* essentially asserts a quest for dominance: "You will want to overcome or overrule your husband—to lead him." It's an obvious reference to the fact that because she had held an equal role, God's new post-Fall edict would be a tough pill for her to swallow. And understandably so, given that an inner sense of equality in dominion was created in both the male and female of the human species (not to mention the fact that both have been given equal creative potential and skills for leading to this day).

But God was establishing a new order, intended for the redemptive process. He was setting it in place—in contrast to the originally arranged creative order that had been violated and rendered dysfunctional. In other words, the man's leading role was not by virtue of creation, but rather was instituted as a provisional part of the redemptive process God set forth.

If one holds that the male is to lead because he is preferred by sovereign choice, the obvious question is: "What is the desired, ultimate objective in this structure of things—benevolent mastery?" Truthfully answered, that can be the only possible conclusion if the original order puts the man over the woman. And such a proposition carries with it a whole trainload of problems, not only where the concept is misapplied, but also in the limits it reaches when it finally arrives at its "best case" goal: half the race is kept at a slightly inferior place.

In contrast, if God assigned the male's leadership role after the Fall as a means of setting forth a redemptive policy, a much higher goal is plainly in view. The target of God's post-Fall assignment of the man's responsibility to lead (not with privileged power or authority, but in the likeness of Christ, who came not to master but to serve) is clearly the recovery of the original order—of both male and female being restored to equal dominion.

Elsewhere I have expanded on this concept, which I believe is not only fully scriptural but ends in accomplishing what we would expect God's redemptive operations to always achieve—the fullest dignity and nobility for every human being who opens to this program of full salvation through His Son, Jesus Christ.

God is at work mightily, targeting the cultivation of a generation of men who keep their commitments, who serve their purpose under Christ and who see their leadership role as servants and not as masters.

I am of the conviction that this "men's awakening" (for it is in motion!) is one of the most pivotal things happening in the Holy Spirit as the new century has been entered.

Fellow leader, go for it! Rise to take your leading role, and as we each do that, expect the end result to be the fullest realization of both men's and women's purposes under God. That's a different agenda than the submersion of one sex at the expense of the other, as though God had ordained one as secondary. Instead, let's lead toward the emergence of men and women as partners unto God's highest destiny for all of us in Christ.

Jack Hayford, "Men First: But for Right Reasons," *Ministries Today* (July/August 1993): 8–9.

Sharpening Your Leading Edge

Where past generations found leaders often intensely concerned with modeling decorum or dignity, or with projecting the raw force of their persona, today's leaders often reflect an inverse picture. By comparison, the cool-headed, casually successful, tousled-hair-and-open-collared corporate mogul is the icon of today's young leader. The contrast depicted seeks to note the reduced place of *passion,* or of manifest *emotion,* on the part of leaders. In short, today's call is for "the cool," and if more than that is in evidence, any one of us is likely to receive an assignment to "chill out."

What follows is an invitation to read about a breakfast meeting...and to consider another meeting—in an upper room. The proposition is clear: To miss the latter is to inevitably be *dulled* as a leader, however "cool."

For More...

A *Passion for Fullness* is my quest to set forth in book form a call to an even-handed, balanced, yet urgent, leadership lifestyle.[11] If the following chapter resonates, this book—which includes testimony of the passion that brought breakthrough in the leadership of leaders like Finney and Moody—may nurture that "hungering and thirsting after righteousness" that Jesus described.

[chapter 11] Time to Lose "Patience" — and Pursue Passion

I was conversing with a young pastor over breakfast. He was in town participating in one of my modules at the Jack W. Hayford School of Pastoral Nurture. As I was enjoyably chewing my usual "burnt to my request" English muffin (well buttered), he asked a particularly timely question, not that it was especially insightful (no reflection on him—I'll call him Chuck) but one that provoked something in me. (That's "provoked" as in "stimulated, awakened, prompted a response," not as in "irritated.")

Because of an unusual slice of history that uniquely relates me to him, I set aside an early breakfast before we headed for the larger gathering of bright leaders we would join for the day. The words were simple, but the look on his face was deeply searching—hoping to find how I, as a leader, thought and processed my life.

"What's your most compelling goal right now?" he inquired, earnestly.

The words ignited synapses, sketching a list on the screen of my mind—goals that are "always," and some "right now":

1. *Always:* to walk with Jesus in faith and purity; to love Anna as a devoted husband; to minister God's Word with power wherever I go; and to serve the staff and family at The Church On The Way as I am often asked to do now in my post-senior-pastor season there.

2. *Right now:* to serve those coming to the School of Pastoral Nurture, not to mention advancing and serving the marvelous growth as God fulfills His call to me to build The King's College and Seminary.

However, I didn't recite any of those abiding goals, nor add to the present ones my media and writing mission. I knew he was really asking for something to help for the grid for processing his own life. He wanted to know:

- ▪ What can you tell me that will help me shape priorities?

- ▪ How can you help me become a more effective pastor and spiritual leader?

- ▪ Where can you point me that will guide the shape and thrust of my ministry?

He's a sharp, sensitive guy—nothing superficial or shallow about him in any way, but so tuned to the usual thought habits of today's leader I felt constrained to move away from and beyond the usual. His expectations were sighted on the kind of thing today's leadership culture and manuals tend to look for—something on the order of, "Give me three goals to target so success—growth—can be gained" (or some other motivational/managerial technique pointing toward achievement).

I sensed his inquiry looking that direction, not because I saw him as less than discerning, but because this quest and the mindset behind it so dominate the landscape in today's church-leader culture.

Leaders in the present North American church often fixate on the notion that what we all need to succeed is to some-how find "a better mousetrap." This tends to produce a relentless quest down endless avenues:

- [■] **Scouring Internet websites**

- [■] **Plowing through leadership material and highlighting slogans in the latest corporate motivational book**

- [■] **Near-frantic idea/program-hunting visits to high-visibility churches**

- [■] **Labored analyzing of contemporary culture and local demographics**

- [■] Diligently processing "makeovers" on everything from the church's platform arrangement to its parking lot signage

These aren't invalid exercises, and I hold no opposition to such sincerely sought, purely motivated quests. However, the majority of the time, they at best prove only temporarily useful, and far too often end in providing little more than a cosmetic for a much deeper need. In short, neither durable change nor spiritual dynamics are likely to ever be gained via the labored means of human ingenuity.

Efforts at *finding and doing things* beget inevitable weariness with having tried so hard and gained so little. And a lot of pastors such as the young man having breakfast with me find a net result reading, "disillusionment," and sometimes, "despair." Leaders need more than a plan, program or procedure—and I was about to add another "p" (and hope it superceded and supported all the foregoing).

More Than a Plan Is Needed

Of course, I recognized that Chuck (my invented name for the bright young shepherd on the other side of the breakfast table) was actually hoping to pick my brain for a plan or a system to "make things work better." And the following chapter, while not "systems" oriented, does provide a move detailed grid for being sure you have "the right stuff" and clearly reveals I *don't* minimize the need for lists, pointers, details and procedures. But Chuck had already been around the block a few times, and he was ready—in fact, needful—of something more. That's why my answer was as follows:

"Chuck," I said, "there are lots of answers to your question, a number of worthy goals I could cite. But to be very frank, I'm becoming less and less patient these days with the idea that a 'corporate or business system' can make a leader or grow a church. Because parallel to the increase of that mindset, to my view, an increased passivity and reduced priority are being placed on what I see as a primary leadership 'must: *passion.*"

He nodded, indicating he was following me, but his eyes also evidenced an uncertainty as to "what exactly" I was referencing. I continued.

"The more I observe today's church leadership, the more I believe an unapologetic passion is needed in two regards: 1) passion in our personal worship of God (then, in the way we lead the flock to do the same); and 2) passion in pursuing an abiding fullness of His Spirit in our lives (then, in wisely

LETTING "IRON SHARPEN IRON"—DISCIPLING THE LEADER'S MINDSET

drawing everyone in the congregation toward the same experience)."

I intoned my words in a way that emphasized the word *passion*. I went on to indicate my impatience with the studied, social reserve I've battled in myself, and equally discovered ingrained in other good but intimidated pastors.

Understanding as I do the varied situations they face—where church controls and people-pressure dare them to lead with passion, I usually take slower steps getting to that point. But I am inclined to lose my patience lately, and I am hoping other leaders might agree, accept and apply my point: There *are* certain *issues* and certain *times* in which *passion ought to preempt patience.*

A Discerning Distinction

I will never defend wild-eyed fanaticism. Nor am I arguing for passion as, for example, a license to carnally indulging anger when things don't happen fast enough. My plea is not to give place to the shallow, selfish pushiness of self-will erupting or manipulating to "get things my way—now!"

To argue for passion is not to indulge in a proposition that patience is supplanted and impatience given a throne in your values or mine. But I have found a law of diminishing return where that order of patience is exercised that becomes so placid, so cooled, so bound by reserve that the status quo is never confronted.

- [■] Whenever I find myself caving in to difficulties instead of opening to new dimensions of God's grace, I need passion, not patience.

- [■] Whenever I find I'm surrendering to the situation instead of making a new surrender to God, I need passion, not patience.

In other words, I'm arguing for a divine discontent, and I related my feelings in a way that Chuck was not only following, but I sensed his confirmation—an acknowledgment that he welcomed the "heads up." He perceived what I'm hoping to relate here with clarity—hoping to help leaders discern and overcome—that so-called "patience" isn't always what it claims to be. It's something else that submits to the rationalizings of fear, doubt, passivity and pride—that believes the lying voice that whispers: "Don't get too excited about God or expect too much of Him. Tough it out. Be patient." That "something else" may run the gamut from false dignity to cowardice, or from unbelief to worldly-mindedness. Because, in fact, the Bible reveals a leadership style that is *moved and moveable:* compassion, passion, tears, indignation. A divine discontent, not a patient passivity, needs to motivate more of me than my culture will ever suggest.

- [■] It is passion, not patience, that moved Jesus through Gethsemane's ordeal and paved the way to Calvary. (See Luke 22:39–46.)

- [■] It is passion, not patience, that brought spiritual breakthrough when effort was made to silence the church. (See Acts 4:23–31.)

- [■] It is passion, not patience, that brought Paul to discover grace sufficient for the satanic battle he was waging. (See 2 Corinthians 12:7–10.)

These, and so many other Bible examples of pure passion, are prompting to us all to move in times like these. They point us to the post-Easter days that led toward the first Pentecost. They prompt us to open our heart's door to relive again the heart-quest of those days when the disciples passionately waited on God for the Holy Spirit.

Partnering Together

Let me encourage you: Whatever you are going through or whatever your personal challenge, whatever your family trials or whatever your economic circumstances, whatever your physical pain or whatever your wearied soul's tiredness, let us partner together to passionately pursue this principle: If with all your heart you truly seek Him, you will find Him. (Take time to study Jeremiah 29:13; Proverbs 8:17; Psalm 63:1–8; Matthew 7:7–8; and Luke 11:5–13.)

Those were the words filling my heart as I spoke with Chuck, and I feel their force again as I write you, fellow servant. Knowing him, I perceived the implications called him 1) to abandon any casual attitude that would tolerate optional degrees of passion in his life and leadership; 2) to never hesitate to lovingly but assertively call his flock to worship; and 3) to refuse to be intimidated about calling, stirring and leading his flock to open up, with passion, to the Holy Spirit.

What of those issues, or others, beckon you?

Stir Up the Gift

For years, I set aside an hour or two on Saturdays, simply to boldly, passionately, with-songs-shouts-tongues-tears-and-strong cryings out to God, keep the waters of my soul from becoming too placid; to keep the cool calculations of my mind from dominating my leadership mindset. I saw and see it as the practical, spiritual response to Paul's injunction to Timothy, "Stir up the gift!" (2 Tim. 1:6). There is no question we need to hear that timeless call issued to that pastor long ago.

I still need the same today, because I live in the grip of this conviction: There is an order of wholeheartedness at the core of our Lord Jesus' commission to all who would be world-changers. He is not only the wonderful "Lamb of God who takes away the sin of the world" (John 1:29). He is also the One who "shall baptize you with the Holy Ghost and with fire" (Luke 3:16, KJV). His clear desire: to ignite our hearts with the flame of heaven's passion and love.

Decades of leading and teaching God's people have not produced in me a reckless excitability, but I have concluded that whatever else, without passion little will be birthed or broken through. "Cool" Christianity will never successfully resist the bonfires of unbelief that intimidate souls, nor the fiery darts of evil assault that rain from today's skies. We can only fight fire with fire.

I shared these thoughts with Chuck, indicating my impatience with the possibility of any priority or proceduralism intruding between a leader's *heart* as a flaming altar and his or her *head* or *hand* as the channels by which thought and touch will reach to the world. And I believe he embraces that priority; that he recognizes it is his, mine and your responsibility to keep "letting it happen as long ago."

It was another century, and at a season of springtime's warming, that a group of leaders were gathered in a room upstairs. They knew their commission to make a difference in their world, but they also had heard their Master's assignment of a prerequisite: Holy Spirit power! And so it was, after days of passionate pursuit, seeking hard after God, and with one accord, that "suddenly there came a sound from heaven, as of a rushing mighty wind...and there appeared to them divided tongues, as of fire, and one sat upon each of them" (Acts 2:2-3).

As Chuck did, would you say it with me now?

Lord, let it fall upon us again!
And again! Amen.

Jack Hayford, "I'm Losing My Patience," *Ministries Today* (May/June 2001): 18-19.

Sharpening Your Leading Edge

To "sharpen" requires a certain amount of grinding, but it doesn't have to be "the daily grind" kind. There is a delight is *pressing against truth*—not in opposition, but in vulnerability to being shaped by it. And there's an equal joy found in taking time to *push against thoughts*—not in rejection, but in having something of their substance press into our souls—shaping as they're sharpened.

The two following articles provide a pair of grids—not exactly "lists," but frameworks of *thought* and *truth*. Though prepared for the context of a pastor's leadership, my experience with business leaders pursuing Christ is that they not only appreciate and enjoy things in this form; they profit from it. So here is a set of values derived from an interviewer's questions as I answer them; joined to a set of gigantic truths "set in order" for thoughtful hearts to review... and to point toward depths and heights of growth in God.

For More...

I can never too highly recommend the works of my dear friend John Maxwell, whose multiple volumes on themes of leadership are renowned. If he doesn't get you from one side, he will from another. For more on being and becoming the leader you want to be, John is unexcelled.

[chapter 12]   The Right Stuff

A recently overheard wisecrack at a dinner table: "Jesus is coming; eat your dessert first!" It wasn't meant irreverently, though some would be sure to take offense, nor do I believe it was said with any intention at making a contemporary commentary on church culture. But it did. Yes, I think so.

Pardon me if this comes across as dour, cynical or dubious about anyone's sincerity other than my own. Because I do believe the vast majority of pastors and church leaders are serious about God, their ministries, characters and solidity in the Word, joined to sanity regarding Holy Spirit-filled life, practice, worship and gift-ministry.

But there's a lot of "dessert first" thinking out there as you scan the horizon of church life. It's everywhere—that looseness of mindset among some that is shaped by short-term goals and solely pragmatic means for seeking a "success" that, by its absence of substance "going in," doesn't take long to "go out."

I heard of one leader acknowledging the "short shelf life" of a technique he had found for drawing crowds, and another disdaining any preaching that utilized a text of more than five verses ("Reading any more Bible than that will lose attention").

Add to this the ease with which exposition is set aside for the sake of "communication," and Internet humor becomes the key to sustaining audience attention in sermons, and the idea of true shepherding—leading and feeding the flock for the long haul—becomes a decreasing concern, except among the thoughtful, the thirsty and those who are hungry for righteousness in an hour that only "kingdom come" will make a truly lasting difference.

I'm very much "into" this arena of concern today, motivated for the most part by my continuing and deepening picture of what pastors are really seeking—that is, the pastors who are truly shepherd-hearted and true servants of Jesus' flock. My exposure every month to another new group of forty to forty-five senior pastors, who always represent a considerable spectrum of age, affiliation, church size, ethnicity and educational background, provides an affirmation.

While a lot of "puff" blows in the Christian media and entertainment realm, and competitors scramble to be acknowledged as the next mega-mogul, the growing evidence is that there are actually a preponderance of pastors willing to "wait for dessert." In other words, they are looking at the issue: "How do I lead in a way that lasts, builds for time, runs in a way as to finish well, serves to grow people, not 'my ministry,' and lives to offer the sacrifice of my life for Christ, not to advance my success under His name?"

It was in the recognition of some of these issues that I received a call from an interviewer recently. The objective was to ask a longtime, durable and fruitful senior to answer questions concerning those very values: "How do you think about life and leadership, in the ways that have contributed to the lasting, the livable and the life-begetting?" For what it's worth, here's the summary of my answers to that interview. Maybe you can use them to spark a discussion among those leaders among whom you fellowship.

Q: What are the marks of a good and faithful pastoral ministry?

A: I would prioritize seven: 1) servant spirit toward people; 2) consistency and fidelity to God's Word; 3) purity in morals and integrity in ethics; 4) commitment in marriage and family; 5) trustworthy and practical in business and finance; 6) hospitable and gracious in relationships; and

7) a heart of compassion for the larger community, both Christian and non-Christian.

Q: What habits and practices do you feel can sustain a good ministry over time?

A: The basics, in my view, are born of the above priorities and are a combination of habits that are both spiritually focused and honest in relationships:

- Pursuit and cultivation of a strong, intimate walk with Christ

- Constant hunger for and growth in the Word of God

- Prioritizing of one's marriage relationship and family life

- Refusal to accrue debt or succumb to a self-serving lifestyle

- Building accountable relationships with a small group of peers

- Choosing to remain unconstrained by opportunism, ecclesiastical separatism or intellectualized vanity

Q: What are the major challenges you see facing pastors in ministry today?

A: With a broad brush, I would note four things, recognizing other issues still remain:

- **Increasing intensity of the spiritual battle, intensified moral temptations and the threats related to a cultural weakening in marriage commitments**

- **Reduced societal respect for the pastoral office, which discourages and begets a sense of reduced worth among leaders**

- **False definitions of success projected by reason of media and mega-ministries, which create illusions for pursuit and monsters of intimidation**

- **General absence of a clearly focused definition of church, its ministry and a pastor's role in cultivating people who truly find their identity in Christ and who are led to minister in His name**

Q: What do you feel are the things that either inhibit or encourage the practice of good ministry?

A: Let me simply note two in each category. First, things that inhibit the practice of good ministry:

- **A lack of prophetic vision and clear focus on our lives and times, leading to a business-as-usual rather than a poised-for-the-moment stance, and a preach/teach-from-the-textbook habit of convenience rather than**

LETTING "IRON SHARPEN IRON"—DISCIPLING THE LEADER'S MINDSET

bothering to seek the mind of the Spirit for one's messages from the Word

[■] A lack of perspective on realities of spiritual conflict (resulting in "wrestling flesh and blood" rather than confronting "principalities and powers"), and a lack of discernment of the true pastoral task of seeking to shape big people more than being trapped in the pursuit of building a big church

Things that encourage:

[■] Holding a broad view of grace, secured in a theology that places worth and value on God's purpose in humankind

[■] Maintaining strength and mutuality with one's spouse, so that your love, companionship, partnership and sense of being called together provide a foundation of conviction about your life and purpose, no matter what

Q: What types of activities that support pastoral ministry need to be expanded?

A: There is a need to move from the traditional dependency upon what I call "professionally focused" conferences to "prophetically focused" gatherings. Pastors and church leaders do need to hone skills, learn methods and cultivate capacities at a business, informational and functional dimension. But these pursuits, as obvious as is their value, too easily distract from those things that are the fundamental essence of ministry. Pastors need, and I believe hunger for, more:

- In-depth interaction with proven pastoral leaders, focusing on the practical and spiritual sides of ministry more than merely the theological and academic sides

- Insight into the keys of vital, sound-minded power-ministry that transcends "a show," and into the ways of vibrant kingdom dynamics for leading a congregation in its prayer, worship, intercessory and ministry life

- Cultivation of fellowship and relationship with fellow pastors in the larger community

It is a thrilling thing to be at the time of life I am (I just turned sixty-eight) and at the time we all are—into a new century, and so near Jesus' return! At such a time, much more is needed than a quick "dessert." Indeed, I have something of an agenda to propose: That the shorter the time we have, the more we need "the right stuff"—the spiritual substance that lasts…and lasts.

The hour is becoming darker and the battle storms more intense. Accordingly, we need "weighty light" amid darkness that can be felt, and we need firm anchoring as the winds of spiritual adversity swirl at hurricane proportions.

Yes, Jesus is coming! As fellow leaders called to "run the race with patience" and to "fight the good fight—faithful unto death," we need to skip the dessert table and check in at the Savior's training table.

Meet you there.

Jack Hayford, "The Right Stuff," *Ministries Today* (September/October 2002): 20–21.

[chapter 13] Truth: The Essential Framework

See two scenarios with me, both in the Pacific Region:

[■] Scores of Filipino leaders are in retreat, gathered from across a nation where—in the south—Muslim guns rattle incessantly and the remembrance of American hostages held for ransom still hangs in the corners of everyone's mind. Their speaker—Sam Webb, a U.S. pastor regarded as an apostolic voice, a nurturer of hundreds of churches, and a trusted, even-handed teacher for over thirty years of faithful life and fruitful service. As he distributes the format for their week of study, prayer and fellowship, they receive a study outline: "The Essentials" —a plain, unapologetic pursuit of what Acts 2 describes as one of the practices which secured the evangelism successes of the early church: "...they continued steadfastly in the apostles' doctrine..." (v. 42).

[■] One of Hawaii's most effective pastors and undeniably most successful church planters—Ralph Moore— is reviewing resources for a new season of training leaders. To meet him is to, at once, find a warm, friendly brother, but an equally intense, no-nonsense man. Things that grow around him are rooted in substance, so it becomes all the more significant to discover him placing an order for several hundred copies of a new handbook of biblical doctrine: *Grounds for Living*.[12] His motive is the same as Sam's—knowing the church is not only grown through evangelism, but established "on the foundation of the apostles and prophets, Jesus Christ Himself being the chief cornerstone" (Eph. 2:20).

Those two scenes prompt two points of personal joy in my soul, each one for a very different reason. The first, I'm gratified whenever I find dynamic leaders who use their influence to apply 1 Timothy 4:6, "If you instruct the brethren in these things, you will be a good minister of Jesus Christ, nourished in the words of faith and of the good doctrine which you have carefully followed." In a day when polls tell us that more than a third of those claiming to be "born again" do not affirm their view of God's Word as containing "absolute truth," Sam and Ralph are certainly securing the turf of their arenas of influence against last days confusion, deception and error. Their tactics aren't defensive, nor do either of them teach "doctrine" to train up a band of arguing, combative, legalistic leaders. But they know that the multiplication of the today's harvest not only needs "good seed," but it must also be founded on solid truth. It's basic—proven wisdom wherever the church not only advances, but is also established. It's essential, whether we serve hundreds of churches as they do, or pastor a single flock as most do.

The second thing that made me feel good about the two scenes above is that both men were using resources of mine: one, "The Essentials" (the outline follows below), and the other, my book *Grounds for Living*. Of course, I feel neither smart nor smug, and I at first hesitated to even mention it, feeling humbled by the fact. But it seemed worthy to observe here, as we look at leadership issues—especially ones that may not be addressed often enough.

Teaching "sound doctrine" is clearly a primary, assigned task for church leaders. Take a trip through the Pastoral Epistles and underscore the issue: 1 Timothy 1:10; 2 Timothy 4:3; Titus 1:9; 2:1—they all use the word *ugianouse,* "healthy or healthful," and thereby establish a principle for all of us who lead today: We are not only called to see individuals and churches *birthed,* but also to teach in ways to assure their long-term *health.* It's something that deserves a new emphasis today, not only because the winds of evil's error are blowing stronger than ever, but also because another trend holds considerable risk.

Everywhere I go today, I'm finding an enchantment among church leaders with the goal of being "effective communicators." And, of course—with the greatest message in the world to deliver, we all want to be that! But within the growing preoccupation to be contemporary, informative, truthful (and even humorous at times), *fullness* of truth and *thoroughness* of teaching seem to be getting short shrift. While I don't believe any pastor/leader would intentionally short-change those he or she leads, I do think the question legitimately belongs on the table today—big time: *When and how will we disciple today's Christian?* Is it possible to do both—be interesting and be thorough, to be a good communicator and still cover essential details? Of course the answer is *yes,* but *what* needs to be covered, and *where* will it fit in the church calendar?

What I offer in the following doesn't answer all the questions that one gives rise to in my mind, but perhaps it will spark a further inquiry into your own perception-of-task, preaching/teaching plan and general approach to discipleship. (Forgive the commercial, but you might consider spending a week with forty-five other pastors at the Jack W. Hayford School of Pastoral Nurture, where more of this subject is explored along with other key pastoral challenges.) In the light of the times we face, and reminded by the model of the two pastors mentioned above, let me offer some food for serious thought regarding the leader's mission to teach.

Deciding What's Really Important

For thirty years of consecutive pastoral teaching with one congregation, I pursued the goal of shaping "ministry-minded believers"; i.e., people whose view of their vocation was that their locations of life and business were their God-given place to let Jesus "do things through them." All pastoral teaching focused on this and sought to answer this question I kept internalized: "Through this week's message, what can I deposit in each person's life that will not only inspire, but that will incrementally increase the deposit of the Word's vital life in them that more of Jesus may be incarnated through them?"

With reasonable regularity I visited themes that I saw as pivotally important to shaping a ministry-minded believer and a spiritually maturing congregation. That pursuit gave us a working *conceptual* grid—Bible-rooted *themes* I presented and applied, usually in short four- to six-week series of teachings. I call this thematic grid "The 24 Concepts of NT Church Life." More recently, I decided to develop a companion framework—a *doctrinal* grid—a structure of the *truths* that undergird the biblical concepts I had taught and preached for years. Basically, I had been teaching "doctrine" according to its original New Testament meaning—*practice, behavior, lifestyle, spiritual conduct.* Now, with this, I have framed a list fashioned after those terms used when the traditional definition of "doctrine" is used—i.e., *theology, foundational truth, spiritual ideas.*

For brevity, I've worded these as concisely as I can. I call them *The Essentials*—i.e., basic biblical building blocks necessary to disciple a people *founded and freed* in the truth of God's Word, and to be led to *fullness and fruitfulness* in the power of God's Spirit. Each awaits "unpacking," just as I have done over the years, to cultivate the health and balance of the individual believer—the person who ultimately is God's strategic person designed to make a difference in our world.

Concerning Divine Revelation

1. *The inspiration and authority of the Holy Scriptures:* **Helping people understand the Bible's supernatural source, absolute authority and its resource for growth and freedom.**

2. *The existence and nature of God and the Godhead:* **Teaching the character of the sovereign God—our Creator and the Sustainer of all things—His worthiness, His ways and His workings.**

3. *The revelation and incarnation of the Son of God:* **Introducing Jesus our Redeemer—from first glimpses in the prophets to His birth, His ministry and His saving work.**

4. *The general witness of the Holy Spirit to all humankind:* **Helping people recognize how the Spirit has been sent to awaken souls to God and to draw them to Christ.**

Concerning Redemption in Christ

1. *The message of the gospel for all the world:* **Spreading the truth of God's love given in His Son Jesus' blood**

atonement for human sin, that "whoever believes in Him will not perish but have everlasting life."

2. *The freedom from guilt and condemnation:* Leading believers to a solid assurance in Christ—knowing God's justifying grace, full forgiveness, abiding love and total acceptance.

3. *The meaning and significance of being a child of God:* Seeing the Father's hope for each of us in Christ—recovering our created intent, entrusting with authority and leading us to triumph.

4. *The issues of sanctification and deliverance:* Nurturing toward freedom and holiness of life—avoiding exaggerations of law or grace, being "cleansed from filthiness of the flesh and spirit."

Concerning Basic Disciplines

1. *The intent and application of the biblical sacraments:* Teaching, beyond ritual, the dynamic intended in water baptism and in our faithful observance of the Lord's Table.

2. *The necessity of nurture through God's Word:* Guiding forward in a practical use of God's holy Word, growing habits of reading, feeding, study and memorization.

3. *The promises and pathway of praying with faith:* How an intimate daily walk with Christ in prayer cultivates love's climate for creative prayer—the appropriation

of God's promises with boldness, humility and biblical confidence.

4. *The knowledge of and obedience to God's will:* Teaching principles for finding the Father's intended personal purpose for one's life, as His Word, will and ways are welcomed.

5. *The principles and practice of stewardship and giving:* Understanding God's call to yield our treasure, time and talents through tithes, offerings and service; learning to abound in His prospering ways unto the blessing of others.

Concerning Spiritual Empowering

1. *The call to and ministry of the baptism with the Holy Spirit:* Leading every believer to receive "power from on high" as Jesus promised; teaching to minister this experience with the same passion and expectation as the early church.

2. *The gifts and fruit of the Holy Spirit:* Teaching the place and operation of spiritual gifts, while growing in the grace and maturation of spiritual fruit; reflecting Jesus' character and charisma in life, ministry and influence.

3. *The purpose and patterns of the prophetic word:* Cultivating wisdom and balance in receiving and responding biblically to the Holy Spirit's gift of "words" of temporal prompting.

4. *The promise and ministry of health and healing:* Leading with biblical love, grace and faith as we open to God's healing covenant and Christ's healing ministry for the whole person—spirit, soul and body.

5. *The realm and ministry of the kingdom of God:* Instructing in the life dimensions opened by Jesus' call to "repent...the kingdom is at hand"; discerning His ongoing call to "reign in life."

Concerning the Church

1. *The mission and structure of the church:* Showing how Christ builds His church locally and globally through His appointed servant-leaders given to grow the member-ministry of His body.

2. *The priorities and practice of Spirit-filled worship:* Leading toward biblical, vibrant personal and corporate worship with a reverent, humble and joyous freedom to enter His presence.

3. *The principles of authority and submission:* Finding the balance of applied submission; how a biblical regard for God-given authority in life opens to fullest freedom and dynamic living.

4. *The dominant value and power of love:* Teaching to know and grow in God's love; learning the grace of this overarching trait of His nature, which values human distinctiveness, remembers human finiteness and shows patience and mercy toward human fallibility.

LETTING "IRON SHARPEN IRON"—DISCIPLING THE LEADER'S MINDSET

Concerning Spiritual Conflict

1. *The origin and nature of Satan and the demonic:* Helping people learn how to resist the devil, break strongholds and cast out demons, without presumption, superstition, fear or confusion.

2. *The reality of the invisible and of angels:* Teaching Christ as "Creator of all things visible and invisible," toward a discerning, functional faith that embraces both realms as equally real.

3. *The call to and means of spiritual warfare:* Equipping in Spirit-enabled intercessory prayer; leading to a sane, scriptural engagement in the age-long battle "in the heavenlies."

4. *The issues of eternal life and eternal loss:* Seeing God's love and benevolent intent in His call and requirements of humankind, with the eternal implications of obeying or rejecting Him.

Concerning Issues of Daily Life

1. *The present prophetic moment:* Teaching the prophetic word of hope revealing the final triumph of God's purpose through His Messiah; His return, millennial rule and eternal promise.

2. *The vocation and ministry of the believer:* Teaching the dignity of each one's gifting and calling within God's

design and creative purpose to extend His life into all human enterprise and experience.

3. *The meaning and responsibility of a witness:* Hearing Jesus' command to love our neighbor, declare the gospel, shine as lights, bear the truth; "salting" the world in all realms—including business, politics, education and the arts.

4. *The divine purpose of God for Israel and the Jews:* Embracing God's "chosen people" whom He has used to initiate and advance redemption's plan throughout their history; relating with biblical sensitivity to their past, present and future.

Concerning Persons and Family

1. *The divine call to biblical manhood and womanhood:* Teaching both genders the Father's unique call and way for male and female believers to live in a society where true humanity is mistaken, confused or neglected.

2. *The God-ordained order for human sexual behavior:* Discipling all regarding God's gift of human sexuality; teaching responsible growth as beings given such a capacity for either lifelong fulfillment or destructive self-indulgence.

3. *The divine design for the home and family:* Training in the principles of foundational relationships; bringing God's order for life in ways that focus, fulfill and bring fruitfulness.

There you have it—*The Essentials*—an outline. It is a measuring stick that calls us to the edge of God's Word, that we may probe with it, pursuing these themes unto deeper depths and higher heights, growing as leaders, that we together:

> **May be able to comprehend with all the saints what is the width and length and depth and height—to know the love of Christ which passes knowledge; that you may be filled with all the fullness of God.**
>
> —Ephesians 3:18–19

Jack Hayford, "What's Really Important," *Ministries Today* (July/August 2001): 20–21.

Section 3

Leading Through the Seasons

Putting an "Edge" on Celebration

A profound reward awaits the leader who shows people the real and worthy way to celebrate. In a world that doesn't understand the difference between celebration and "partying," the practice of some is either to withdraw or to criticism—to avoid any level of participation or to comment cynically regarding the superficiality that offends them.

God is the Father of true celebration, and there is a dynamic and fulfilling "edge" that can be restored where needed. Having been raised in an ordinary family with no extraordinary means to allow pursuing celebration except the wealth of understanding the season as my parents nurtured us, I naturally came to see the value of "leading" from season to season, from holiday to holiday.

It is undoubtedly a tribute to that mood of celebration characterizing my upbringing that has so flavored the season and holidays that something "prophetic" seems to come upon me in anticipating them. The selected poems that follow, preceding each article, are that—prophetic statements! I hope they stimulate something of the mood, passion and color of each—but with that, awaken something of mission, praise and celebration!

Further, I hope than any leader—involved in any arena of leadership—might profit from "a pastor's pen at the seasons of our celebration." There are pathways here to be walked in any environment; pathways upon which deeper meaning is found as richer dimensions of the season are noted, observed and applied.

Note

The poetic introduction to each chapter is not accompanied by the usual "For More..." entry of resources. However, two general ones might be noted.

Rebecca Bauer's award-winning book *The 25 Days of Christmas* was written for adults to read and to share with children.[13] Also, her equally magnificent work *Seasons of Praise* masterfully ties fifty-two hymns and songs of worship to the weeks and seasons of the year.[14]

Living Way Ministries also has an online catalog of my seasonal preaching, which has become a rich resource for leaders who preach or speak, and great inspiration for those who simply want to find refreshing insights to enrich a savoring of the seasons (www.livingway.com).

Sharpening Your Leading Edge

Considering the marvel of this season's colors, it all seems to be a summons to celebrate the depth of our Creator's love.

Autumn Hillside

Autumn's hillside panorama, multicolor-spangled lace,
Leave me awestruck by Your wonders, mighty God of
time and space.
I am humbled and rejoiced to say I know the One who
made
All the sparkling, splashing splendor I see everywhere
displayed.

Lakes reflect bright banks of color—rivers ricochet
with light,
As the mix of mists announce that summer's sun is
taking flight.
Greyish clouds are riding breezes, spreading firefall all
around,
And mid leaves of flaming color, here I bow—knees to
the ground.

Where I stood as stunned to feel the color-thunder of
the Fall,
Now I've knelt—for one grand wonder gleams to me
within it all.
Hillside flame has burst, exploding glowing truth
within my mind—

Suddenly I see Your Love amid these colors You've combined.

Heaven's palette brushing landscapes lavishly with lighted Love,
Paint the hills in shades that shout to share Your message; teaching of
Your grand mystery eternal—how the wisdom of Your ways
Has transcended human brokenness with Your amazing grace.

See! The season speaks in splendor—all in *purples, reds* and *golds;*
Shades that summarize the glory of the story Love unfolds:
How in grace You left heav'n's purple robes for Calvary's scarlet red,
So the Fall of man might realize a golden gift instead.

Now You've made each leaf a message 'mid this rich autumnal show,
Pointing to Your Tree of Life and saying, "Come, bathe in the glow—
From the darkness of your wanderings or the dullness of your pain,
From the deadness of your endings to My glory-gilded gain."

Hear these rustling reminders that His endings all are bright,

Whisp'ring, "Heaven's dawn will one day burn away
this world's long night."

Saying, "See the grace in purple!" Calling, "See the love
in red!"

Lifting, "Stand where you have fallen—here's a golden
gift instead!"

We need ask no more why autumn seems to waken
such a yearning,

For the answer's clear—it's glory calls us each to a
returning;

To recall our hearts to childhood, singing, "Come, roll
in those leaves;

And be clothed in all the beauty God's grand Autumn
Hillside gives."

So I stand, my soul aflame, ignited by this glory rare,

As with joy I've opened to the autumn hillside message
there.

Now bright-clothed with Love's salvation, I've the hope
all autumns bring:

Past earth's endings—*New beginning;* past earth's
winters—*Endless spring.*

JACK W. HAYFORD

OCTOBER 2000

[chapter 14] The Blessings of Autumn

It was September 21—the first day of autumn. That morning I awakened to a special sense of God's presence in the room. I was just on the brink of my sixtieth birthday, and Proverbs 4:18 had come to my heart with a special warmth and richness of promise: "The path of the just is like the shining sun, that shines ever brighter unto the perfect day." The prospect of stepping into my first decade of "latter years" had not troubled me, but God's Word seemed to prompt a special welcome to their high hope and bright promise.

Minutes later, as I was at my morning devotions, a sudden sweep of *expectancy* washed over me as that verse's truth began to glow within my spirit. *How like our Creator,* I thought, *filling the "autumn of our years" with promise!* And that instant, like a distant echo from a high, heavenly plateau, unconjured by mere human imagination, I heard a Voice—deep within—whispering, "I am going to bring you the blessings of autumn. It is your loveliest season and one always filled with continued harvest and the most beautiful holidays."

My eyes misted with the moment, for I felt the immediacy and personal attentiveness of the Father's care toward me so profoundly I hardly could find words to adequately respond in praise for His love—a gracious, mighty and superintending love, watching over me, going before me. Shortly, I took my journal in hand and began to write my impressions of the moment, and I also logged a kind of "teaching" I felt I was being given—one for me personally, but perhaps useful for others as well.

A Thanksgiving Delivery

It was only eight weeks later—*Thanksgiving Day! My favorite of all holidays!* Among the special qualities of that day, I treasure the early morning worship service at our church— a gathering that has become a warm tradition for thousands of our congregation. As I walked from the sanctuary, having just concluded that annual event of high praise, deep thanksgiving, victorious testimonies and very touching interaction among the whole church family, I was met by my assistant. "Call Doug," she said. "He has just taken Christa to the hospital—they think she has begun labor!"

Our youngest daughter and her husband lived about two hundred miles away and were expecting their first child—but not for nearly another three weeks. I found Anna, who was still hugging a host of members in the sanctuary, and told her about the call. We both felt excitement, but the earlier-than-expected onset of labor could also be reason for concern. We both smiled and waved to others of the congregation as we hurried to my office, phoned and were quickly assured by our son-in-law that the doctor gave no reason for concern.

The baby was born about four hours later—a thumping more-than-seven-pound boy—his birthweight providing solid evidence that he wasn't premature! And he had arrived on Thanksgiving Day!

Arguing Against Childlikeness

Later that day I was musing over the joys of the day—especially over the birth of our grandson—when a thought probed the corners of my mind—one I, at first, was inclined to dismiss. *Could it be...since He knows this day is my favorite?* I speculated, but almost instantly dispensed with the "emotionalistic" notion and quickly gave place to cool, human reasoning. *No, Jack!* I thought to myself. *Don't be so juvenile as to even think it. God didn't cause the delivery of the baby on this specific day for your sake!*

But I was jarred by an internal reprimand, one that demanded I answer these questions: "Who is the author of life?" "Who oversees the timing of birth and death when He is trusted as Lord?" "Who has called us *not* to the cool reasonings of human intellectualism and its companion, doubt, but instead invited us to come as children—and believe in His love, His promise, His personal care for us?"

I was being brought to an accounting for my own fears, which argued that "while God is loving and good, it would be too much to think that His love and goodness made such arrangements as these." While facing the reality and simplicity of God's gentle grace and merciful loving-kindness, I humbled my soul to confess the fear-borne pride that hesitates to receive the tenderness of the Father's graces. Just as I did, again, that Voice was there: "Why did you doubt? I told you, 'I am going to bring you the blessings of autumn!'"

It was more than I could contain. Praise overflowed my heart and filled my mouth with song—"Loving-kindness, loving-kindness, His loving-kindness, O how great!" And that could well have been the end of it, and it would have certainly been enough. But "the blessings of autumn" prompting to my heart from the Father's wasn't done with its harvest of loving-kindnesses from Him to me.

Nearly a Year Later

It was fully eleven months later, the following October, and Anna and I had taken a drive into the San Bernardino Mountains to enjoy the fall foliage in Oak Glen's six-thousand-feet-high majestic woodlands. While there, sampling the apple harvest, salivating over scrumptious hot apple pie à la mode and delighting in the colors of the season spangling the narrow valley, we slipped into a small art studio. It was there that we discovered a painting by Thomas Kinkade and were struck not only with the golden splendor of the canvas, but also moved especially by its title: *The Blessings of Autumn*. We had never seen it before, and we were at once captivated by its brilliant artistry evoking every autumnal emotion, as well as the name of the piece and the special meaning it held for us.

The copy at the gallery was sold, so we placed a reservation for our own and awaited word of its availability. In the meantime, Anna was sharing with a friend about our excitement over the painting when surprisingly—and with a

LEADING THROUGH THE SEASONS—PUTTING AN "EDGE" ON CELEBRATION

certain awkwardness—the friend suggested that we cancel the reservation. "Forgive me," she apologized, somewhat amazed herself, "but I happen to know there are plans for *that exact painting* to be presented to you as a gift." She naturally didn't name the party, but by reason of her intimacy with us had been asked by someone else, only days before, if she thought it would be something we would like. Knowing our affection for the autumn season (but not the story of God's "Blessings…" personal prompting to me), she urged the individuals to proceed if they wished.

Just two weeks later a young couple came to our home, bringing the magnificence and color of *The Blessings of Autumn* and presented it to us. "In gratitude," they explained, "for your fruit-bearing influence and mentoring in this just-passed first decade of our own pastoral ministry." We were overwhelmed by their love—and *stunned* by the magnitude of their gift.

But "staggered" better describes what happened next, for the passage of just twelve more days brought the arrival *of a second gift copy of the same painting!*

Can you believe it? It was exactly Thanksgiving Day again!

It was now *exactly* a year to the day since the baby's birth that had come as a heavenly timed reminder of God's good grace—promising forthcoming years of continued fruitfulness, family happiness and holiday joys. Now, as I had walked into my office following our Thanksgiving morning worship service, there before my eyes was propped the painting. Attached was a love note from yet another young pastoral couple: "Pastor Jack and Anna—For the years you have blessed us!"

I Won't Forget—Don't You!

I was bewildered as I drove home, wondering what would we do with two paintings. How could I explain to the second couple? I was feeling so deeply moved, thinking, *No one could deserve such lavish kindnesses,* when the Voice spoke a third time. "These paintings are to indelibly impress the words of My promise upon your heart that I have committed to bring you the blessings of autumn." The impression was clear: He had arranged for us to have two—one in the parsonage and the other at our writing retreat—"So you won't forget!"

So it is that both—our valley dwelling provided by the church and the getaway site Anna and I have for rest, relaxation and writing—radiate the brightness of *The Blessings of*

LEADING THROUGH THE SEASONS—PUTTING AN "EDGE" ON CELEBRATION

Autumn—rendered by Thomas Kinkade, "the Painter of Light," whose creative gifting is used to inspire so many. But most of all, we marvel over how they were arranged for us by *the* Creator—"the *Master* of Light."

He used two precious couples to overflow our hearts with dual, providentially timed reminders of His Word: *"... brighter and brighter unto the perfect day."* What a promise, summoning us all to welcome the wonder-filled love and the promise of eternal joys He offers as we walk with and serve His Son, *the Light of the world.*

Our Father went to special lengths to get my attention and press me with unique evidences and loving reminders so I would not forget it. I've shared it—not as a testimony to any worthiness on my part, but one to the loving-kindness of *Him.*

I won't forget. Don't you, either, for He loves each of us equally. The Creator of autumn's wonder knows how to color our years with His abundant mercies and overflowing goodness.

Jack Hayford, "The Blessings of Autumn," *Ministries Today* (September/October 2001): 18–19.

Sharpening Your Leading Edge

I consider it a part of my pastoral mission to lead people to bring GREAT thanksgiving—mindful of the fact the Father delights in us...and in our praise.

A Gift of Thanksgiving

Ah, Lord, we bring praise and honor
  as a gift of thanksgiving to You.
For Your great grace and Your strong loving-kindness
  now invite our gratitude anew.
So, Lord, we come empty handed,
  lifting only our hearts with our voices—
Now we sing to express gratitude with humbleness
  For the way You provide, ever guide and always
    bless.
We give thanks for the way
  You delight to delight us each day.

Ah, Lord, ev'ry tree and mountain
  rise up with a witness to You.
Fruitful fields speak of Your unchanging goodness,
  and Your mercy sparkles in the dew.
Wind, rain, falling leaves of autumn,
  winter snow, springing flow'rs and the sun,
    shine

Forth the light of Your love, countless blessings from
    above
  As from season to season in You we live and
    move—
Moved to praise You always
  For the brightness You pour on our way.

Great God, as a gifted nation
  we have tasted Your bounty and grace.
So we bow now with this gift of thanksgiving
  to present our worship and our praise.
Dear God, hear our prayer for mercy
  as our song of thanksgiving we raise, pray—
Now forgive us, O Lord. Lead us forward by Your Word.
  By the pow'r of Your hand, spread Your grace
    across our land,
That we ever may be
  Thankful people of praise unto Thee.

JACK W. HAYFORD

NOVEMBER 1986

[chapter 15] The Heart (and Shadow) of Thanksgiving

THANKSGIVING days are often chilled by the changes that autumn brings. We can face such seasons of the soul knowing God's goodness toward us is unchanging.

Grab a cup of whatever and sit with me for a minute, OK?

Allow me to set a coffee/tea table with a double service of this season's moods and the message it speaks if you listen. (At least it's what I hear as I do!) First, here's a remembrance that brought my Thanksgiving gratitude to an even deeper level. Second, here's a brief inspirational piece that sprang from that memory.

A Remembrance

I was thinking about Thanksgiving—my favorite holiday, thinking again of how deeply moved I am at this season. From beholding the *glory* of the autumn season, to reviewing the *glories* of our Creator-Father's multiple goodnesses to us, right on down to the *goodies* on the celebration table around which the family gathers.

Amid my reverie I was caught by the remembrance of a letter from Marti, a woman Anna and I met on a European cruise not long ago. It was between Thanksgiving and Christmas last year that she wrote, sharing her deep sense of gratitude to God, and what she related, simply and without affectation, brought both of us to tears.

The letter contained nothing even remotely dismal or self-pitying. To the contrary, Marti's letter was laden with a positive, upbeat recitation of how genuinely happy she was for God's goodness to her. She elaborated all this, notwithstanding the facts that contextualize her life.

Marti's husband is an alcoholic. He is totally ridden with disease now and has been fighting lung cancer for more than a decade. Though reason would argue he should have been gone long ago, she was filled with the essence of the Thanksgiving season.

She wrote to share with us her overwhelming praise to God for His presence and strength, saying, "I so thank God for the way He fills me with love for my dear Chuck as I love and care for him, even though there's nothing we can really do together—other than wait." She was filling that "waiting" with a "will" to see God's hand of goodness in her circumstance and a "wonder" over how He was doing exactly that!

The whole of her situation has been filled with seeming constancy in the recurrence of necessary surgeries, has overflowed with debilitating difficulties, has been beset by ceaseless financial challenges, and with it all the whole horrible gamut of things that can attend a protracted struggle with terminal disease. Notwithstanding it all, Marti radiates thanksgiving—it shone from her card and letter just as we saw it shine from her face when we spent two weeks with her on a vacation cruise. She is a study in joyous, unselfish, servant-hearted lovingness—and all that without a tinge of pretension, self-pity or self-righteousness.

Caught as I was, on the hook of that memory of Marti, I was moved to write what follows. It's a salute to those who live in "The Shadow of Thanksgiving"—that grand host of devoted believers who remain unshaken by the tremors of upset and upheaval. Though navigating stormy waters, they live in a light that no darkness can diminish. They have a way of helping us all keep perspective by the way they face up to the toughest things life can bring, yet remain people we're happy to be around, people who out-thank many of us who have far less demanding circumstances.

The Shadow of Thanksgiving

The splendor of the Thanksgiving season shines never so splendidly as it does in places and in hearts where the shadows of pain or disappointment are unable to dim the radiance of praise to God. Notwithstanding trials they're traversing or the difficulties being navigated, a multitude of souls are possessed by a wisdom this Thanksgiving Day that is rooted in the reality of God's unchanging goodness.

These heroes of thanksgiving know that because He has never been nor ever will be the source of their struggles, there is never reason to cease worshiping Him. Their praise is unstinted because they laud God's faithfulness to them even though present stresses would test that resolve.

Just as the angle of late autumn's sun casts longer shadows in our hemisphere, so there are seasons of our soul that introduce events and eventualities that stretch traces of darkness across otherwise bright days. And just as November's fogs often dampen our mornings, so this season bespeaks how life's transitions seem to block the sun for today or blur our vision of tomorrow.

But there is a breed of believer that never relents praising—come fog or shadow. This Thanksgiving they're at tables where their praise will rise to God for His multitudinous mercies, bountiful blessings, unflagging faithfulness and glorious goodnesses everywhere. Even though less discerning souls may hear their words of thankfulness for their blessings, and looking cautiously around at the praiser's circumstance may whisper, "Where?", their sincerity summons us to see with their eyes of faith and to sing with their heart of praise.

Even when the checkbook balance is small and there is little to nothing in the cupboard. Even when work has evaporated and the heat of the circumstantial is near boiling. Even when strength seems gone, health is waning, and the diagnosis demands dismay. Even when a loved one lingers on the edge of eternity and their lot is to nurse patiently the dying.

Today, let's take our cue from these people whose praise to God—however appropriately prompted by great blessings—is just as praise-ready when shadows come. They're this way because their praise has found its deepest root in the abiding goodness of God's nature, not merely in the temporal goodness of His providence. So join me in this, would you?

LEADING THROUGH THE SEASONS—PUTTING AN "EDGE" ON CELEBRATION

Let's become so fixed in gratitude for the changeless fact that God is good that our praise persists even when transient facts tempt us to transient faith. Yes, join me in the settled will to let the abiding truth of one text gain an inescapable grip on our souls:

> **Every good gift and every perfect gift is from above, and comes down from the Father of lights, with whom there is no variation or shadow of turning.**
>
> **—JAMES 1:17**

A pair of decades ago, a pop lyric sentimentalized on the "Shadow of Your Smile," as one lover sang of his devotion, even in his loved one's absence, saying, it "will color all my dreams and light the dawn." It's not a bad beginning for a hymn this Thanksgiving season, for the changeless Lover of our souls—seen clearly for who He is—deserves our highest praise and deepest devotion. Even when shadows come.

> **Things may change, but He never does;**
> **Tides turn back, but He never will;**
> **Turmoil churns, but He is my peace;**
> **Troubles come, but He's present still.**
>
> **—JACK W. HAYFORD**

This season—any *season!*—may we all rise and sing in the light of this truth about our Father. Even if there's a shadow on your pathway, rejoice, Dear One. Your life is still secured—within the grander shadow of His wings.

It's never dark there.

Jack Hayford, "The Heart of Thanksgiving," *Ministries Today* (November/December 1998): 22.

Jack Hayford, "The Shadow of Thanksgiving," *Ministries Today* (November/December 1998): 23.

Sharpening Your Leading Edge

Creating a Christmastime lyric—for opening each Sunday morning in December—gave an opportunity to take one of the "holiest" songs and sanctify this high season of great celebration—all that Jesus came!

Holy, Holy, Holy

Holy, holy, holy—Lord God Almighty;
Early Christmas morning we rise to worship Thee.
Bright our hearts rejoicing, now this wonder voicing—
God, come in flesh—in Christ Your love we see.

Holy, holy, holy—Lord God Almighty;
Who by prophets spoke proclaiming Christ-Messiah's
> birth.
In Your grace and favor, promising a Savior—
That we might know Your peace and love on Earth.

Holy, holy, holy—all the earth shall praise Thee
For Your heart of love has reached and giv'n Your Son
> for us.
Christmas gift from heaven—all may be forgiven,
Through Jesus' Cross and mercy justified.

Holy, holy, holy—all who hear, sing "Holy!"
For the Holy One of heaven invites us to receive.
Open to salvation! Enter new creation!

Eternal life for all who will believe.

Holy, holy, holy, Lord God of ages,
Once again this Christmastime we lift our songs to
Thee.
Heralding our Savior—Jesus, Earth's Redeemer,
Lamb of the Cross and Lord eternally.

JACK W. HAYFORD

CHRISTMAS 2000

[chapter 16] Making the Holidays Happy and Holy

I love the holidays! All of them! I unabashedly feast on Thanksgiving Day and scream cheers at the TV during the New Year's Day bowl games. As for Christmas, everything brings excitement and joy! After decades of celebrating the holidays, I've learned that celebration is not only fulfilling, but it also brings life, faith and congregation.

Unfortunately, it's not easy to even *get* some Christians to rejoice. Inhibitions abound. Preoccupying burdens of duty dampen souls and tempt a Scrooge-like "humbug"—even from many saints. But I consider helping my flock to release the spirit of rejoicing one of my primary callings at holiday time.

"Rejoice!" Paul commanded the Philippians, and then he immediately repeated himself: "And again I say *rejoice!*" I've often thought that while dictating those words, the apostle mused, *If I only say it once, those dear ones in Philippi will fly on by it and miss taking action.* Then, turning to the amanuensis to whom he was dictating the epistle in a Roman cell, he said, "Write that again: *Rejoice!*"

This isn't hype—it's hope, anchored in the permanent ground of God's fulfilled promise, not in cheap promotionalism or fancy verbiage.

Help every one of your flock to reflect the glory and resound the joy of the angels' song: "Gladness is today's news! A Savior—to you—*today!*" Let's lead our people to celebrate in a way that makes Jesus' love appealing to a love-starved and joyless culture. Some sincere saints see the holidays as a time to attempt to impose something godly on their relatives. Instead, let's simply expose them to the raw reality of unhampered happiness. Let your light shine and His love overflow in a loving and sensitive way.

Of course, our celebration starts with a clear focus on the Lord. "Sanctify—give special place to—the Lord in your hearts, always ready to show others the reasonableness of the hope that fills your life!" (1 Pet. 3:15, author's paraphrase). That verse, prompting our witness to an inquiring world, is especially applicable to our traditional year-end holidays. I can't imagine anything more likely to open hearts to Christ than being exposed to the joy of Jesus in a home or congregation where people have learned to make the holidays *happily holy.* The world notices the difference between our true festive joy and its own hollow efforts at celebration. Sanctify the Lord God *first*—center everything around Him, worshiping with joyous song and featuring the timeless Word of His truth. Then *rejoice!* Let people learn what it's like to live in the liberty that the *truth* and *Spirit* of Christmas really bring.

Sanctifying the season—making holidays happily holy—doesn't require that we trash traditions to prove our piety. God's grace in us not only brings personal progress in purity, but His Holy Spirit within us has the power to infuse every part of life with beauty and blessing, if we'll let Him. This means that amoral traditions may be taken by believers and converted to happy and holy occasions.

Giving presents can relive the story of the wise men and remind us that we serve a gift-giving God. A Christmas tree can represent the coming of the Light into the world and remind us that the greatest gift of all was given to us on a tree, ushering out death and bringing us forgiveness, regeneration and eternal hope.

Such conversion of tradition to meaningful observance is

not a concession or compromise. It is sad that so many sincere believers have had the life "wrung out" of Christmas through the debunking tirades of people afraid of simple happiness. Rather than fleeing the innocent cultural traits of celebration, let's "ring in" the season by choosing to fill our culture's habits of celebration with deeper color, purifying them by our enlightened perspective and radiating them with a richness of joy that only the original Spirit of Christmas can bring.

From Thanksgiving on, make your home and church a center of welcome to those who are hungry—whether for food, family or fellowship. When people's mouths are satisfied with good things and their souls are stimulated with signs of seasonal joy, then their hearts will open to the One who is central to it all. Let's teach our people by example. Let the feasting of the holidays feed others with *every* delight—a testimony of joy that ignites hope and faith in a dreary world that only knows the momentary "kick" of a raucous office party or a bottle of bubbly.

Jack Hayford, "Making Holidays Happily Holy," *Ministries Today* (November/December 1990): 30.

Sharpening Your Leading Edge

Each Christmas the sudden splash and spread of lights on our streets, store windows, rooftops and trees shout aloud: The Light has come! Once more, the testimony to this truth shines everywhere—even where misunderstood or not believed!

The Light Has Come

The Light has come, and the darkness can
    never be the same—O alleluia!
The Light has shone, and the darkness ran
    never to return—O allelu!
Your Word made flesh; Your glory revealed;
    its entrance gave great light.
You spoke; He came; Christ Jesus His name,
    and He has scattered our night.
The Light has come, and the darkness can
    never be the same—O alleluia!
And now the Light shines to every man—
    You can live in Light—O allelu!

The sound of joy fills the earth and sky,
    and the bells peel forth their alleluia!
The day has dawned, and the sun climbs high
    for the Light has come—O allelu!
This Child now born, Himself is the truth;

the truth that sets men free.
His glory shines to all of mankind,
   and His Light brings liberty.
The sound of joy fills the earth and sky,
   and the bells peel forth their alleluia!
With freedom's song lift your voice and cry,
   Jesus Christ is Lord—O allelu!

A silver beam splits the sky above,
   and His star appears—O alleluia!
A glory streams spreading hope and love
   as Messiah comes—O allelu!
He tramples darkness under His feet—
   His battle flag unfurled.
Despair and bondage shatter and flee,
   for He's the Light of the world.
A silver beam splits the sky above
   and His star appears—O alleluia!
His kingdom come is a rule of love
   casting out all fear—O allelu!

The Light has come and to ev'ry man
   Life has been revealed—O alleluia!
Though some resist it, they never can
   overcome its pow'r—O allelu!
For God in flesh once walked on the earth
   as Jesus, Son of man.

The splendor of His glory displayed

continues ages to span.

The Light has come and to ev'ry man

Life has been revealed—O alleluia!

And as it comes unto me, I can

be renewed in Life—O allelu!

JACK W. HAYFORD

CHRISTMAS 1987

[chapter 17] Finding Balance in Our "Christmasing"

How do we make Christmas joyously special without it becoming either paganized or too commercial? I have grown more and more concerned with that question over the years, and I am more deeply convinced than ever that denial of Christmas fun is not required by us who share the deepest faith of Christmas.

Our challenge as shepherds of souls is to find and show the way to a holy and happy celebration of the season.

Sadly, I've encountered many victims of "sanctified Scroogism." I've become wearied by those debunkers whose stock-in-trade is assailing every fun-filled facet of Christmas. On the proposition that God, truth and holiness are threatened by so many of the just-plain-fun features of our culture's Christmas traditions, it's not hard to find sincere souls who:

> ▪ Don't allow their children to give or receive Christmas gifts because "to do so would be a surrender to the superficial commercialism, which misses the point of

the spiritual depth of the occasion."

- Attack everything from "The Night Before Christmas" (written by a devoted pastor, incidentally) to "Frosty the Snowman" on the grounds that these fictionalized representations will become confused in a child's mind with the miracle story of the Babe in the manger.

- Exhaust every effort to renew their attack on the December twenty-fifth celebration date, inasmuch as "no one knows the actual date of Jesus' birth—not really!" And, "Don't you know this wintertime festivity is only a modernized adaptation of the old pagan ritual Saturnalia—satanic to its root?"

- Lambaste Santa Claus as a demon-inspired figure whose mission is to distract us from Christ and infect the mind of every child with the idea that both he and God are merely imaginary personalities.

And the beat goes on—a "beating" that has left in the wake of its assault a much larger contingent of battered souls than blessed ones. Since we've dedicated ourselves for decades to joyous, spiritually minded, Bible-centered, colorful, light-spangled "Christmasing," I've watched too many people get saved and healed to doubt the wisdom of such celebration.

Sure, the silly, superficial and senseless surround us everywhere at this holiday season. But at the same time, there is an incredible vulnerability that manifests in most people from Thanksgiving through year's end. I've picked up the pieces of too many mangled souls to believe that the "anti-Santa, anti-celebration, anti-happy" program works. I can't begin to number those who've told me or have written me about turning from the Lord because of the way their church or parents attacked the joys of Christmas celebrations. Nor can I number the souls who have been swept into eternal life in the midst of our congregation's high and festive times of rejoicing at this season. We even have a night we sing carols—including secular songs. And people receive Jesus in that happy setting—some of them frankly admitting they had no idea that the love of God and the fun of Christmas could be married in a holy union.

Santa himself is a case study in how we can convert culture to serve spiritual objectives. Whatever argument might be mustered against a commercialized Christmas centered in a secular Santa, I still like the old guy. And the reason is that he was "converted" at our house when I was kid—"saved" to serve our family's priorities, which never diverted from Jesus. None of us kids—and none of Anna's and mine (or our grandkids, for that matter)—were ever confused about who the principal personality was in Christmas. We were never in danger of thinking the family fun, secrets and teasing about Santa were in the same league as the family's worship, singing and conversations about the glorious fact that "unto us this day a Savior is born, who is Christ the Lord!"

I've carried into my pastoral leadership the conviction that such traditions can be applied without allowing worldly-mindedness to clutter our celebrating. A pastorally led congregation that embraces Christmas, rather than embarking on a crusade against it, will do more than avoid traumatizing kids by trampling on traditions. This reactionary posturing is worse than "scrooging," not having a ghost of a choice at accomplishing anything lasting other than breeding bitterness and turning people off toward the church. But a church family can convert many of our cultural traditions to serve the interests of evangelism and spiritual training.

Santa is a dramatic emblem of a world crying out for a larger-than-life daddy who will love his kids even when they are not perfect—and give them gifts to fulfill their longings. He's called "Father Christmas" in British Commonwealth nations, and at the holiday season, most of this planet softens up to acknowledge its need of Someone like him. And, of course, that Someone is the real Father of Christmas—"the God and Father of our Lord Jesus Christ"— who perfectly supplies the full answer to humankind's universal longing for a loving and giving father: "For God so loved the world that He gave..."

My Christmas prayer for those of us who lead is threefold:

- [■] **I pray for the wisdom of God—that we might discern the times and seasons and perceive the possibilities of penetrating our culture, rather than attacking it. That's the gist of what the Incarnation is about.**

- [■] **I pray for the spirit of all celebration—the Holy Spirit—to help us prophesy like Zacharias, give like the wise men, shout like the angels and sing like Mary.**

- [■] **I pray that the truth of Christmas becomes a liberating one, filled with the warmth of the Father's family love and overflowing with the joy of Jesus spreading a holy contagion over everything we do.**

Jack Hayford, "Finding Balance in Christmas Celebration," *Ministries Today* (November/December 1991): 24–25.

Sharpening Your Leading Edge

We lead our people each New Year's Eve to renew faith and hope through a service of confession at the Lord's Table and expectation through written "Letters to the Lord"—fixing our hope in Him. While I actually wrote this by the title "Thru' This One Day" on my birthday in 1987, I adapted it for any year.

Into This Year I'd Walk With Thee

Into this year I'd walk with Thee,
Lord Jesus Savior, God to me;
And with each moment let there be
Thy fullness, love and life in me
With Holy Spirit liberty.

Into this year I'd walk with Thee
Thou blessed Lamb of Calvary;
That Thy Cross may my portion be,
And self be slain that men may see
The loving One who died for me.

Into this year I'd walk with Thee,
Thou mighty Christ of Galilee;
And with each step may others see
Thy healing power revealed in me;
May I reflect Thy victory.

Into this year I'd walk with Thee,
Thou Conq'ror of Gethsemane;
That in each choice confronting me
Your will be done with certainty
And God be glorified in me.

Into this year I'd walk with Thee,
Thou Master of eternity;
This heart preserve in purity
That on that morn Thy face I see,
I'll just and unashamed be.

JACK W. HAYFORD

1987

[chapter 18]   Into New Year's—
With Faith and Expectancy

I could hardly believe the "word" came so soon—it was only March, and still nine months to the next new year, when the Holy Spirit prompted my thoughts with this: "Next year is to be the Year of Revelation." And with that, I received a clear sense of pastoral direction, an "overlay" of prophetic vision that will influence the life and pace of our congregation for an entire year.

It has been more than fifteen years since I was first led to seek the Lord for a general, overarching "word" for the upcoming year. That began an annual pattern of seeking something of "the Lord's view" of our body life for each approaching new year in two arenas. My experience has proven that what He gives us as we seek Him turns out to be a dual "word"—both corporate and personal.

My aim has been to sense the Great Shepherd's heart. First, for the whole church family—that is, the small part of His global flock I'm charged to oversee. Second, I want something that can ignite scriptural truth in a way that will bring a spiritual and practical focus for each member of the church, too. Interestingly, with these two immediate pastoral benefits realized by means of seeking God's "thematic counsel" (a biblical, prophetic look at His purpose toward, among and through us), a serendipity has distilled as well. It has not been unusual that certain features of the "theme" have become traits of the general work of God in broader parts of the global body of Christ. Through the year, reports of His moving and working seem so very much like what we are experiencing—and clearly, fulfilling things one might expect to occur by reason of the outflow of the "thematic word."

So it is that I seek and open to the Holy Spirit in this way—each year. I want to "hear what the Spirit is saying to the church." What manner of thrust, what order of concern, what vision for ministry is central to the Father's heartbeat? Or, at least, what particular issue would He have me address in His name?

Since I have made it a pastoral policy to seek to "tune in" to the Great Shepherd's heart and the Spirit's word, I have regularly been rewarded with a distinct sense of direction. As a result, I have presented "themes" for most years; some, for example, have been Year of Refinement, Year of Redemption, Year of Refreshing, Year of New Creation, Year of Salvation, Year of Multiplication, Year of Promise and Patience.

Our pastoral team's response to these has *not* been to make them controlling guidelines or program-dictating requirements to which departments must conform. But they have seemed to provide a basic impetus—a cohesive sense within our church staff and family, begetting an expectancy and earnestness. It flavors each new year with a renewed quest for God's best for their lives, while alerting us to the Word of God that is taught on the subject.

Some years we have presented no "word" at all, for if no direct prompting is forthcoming, we feel no obligation to verify our "insight" by coming up with something. The biblical promise of God's presence is no less real at those times, so no void is felt if the year hasn't a prophetic theme. However, when one is set forth, there are a number of principles that govern my leadership approach to implementing the theme.

1. **I introduce the theme with a short teaching series early in January. This provides a strong biblical basis for the concept.**

2. I always make clear that this word is only as applicable to each individual as the Holy Spirit makes it to them. In other words, no one needs to feel he is less spiritual, unbelieving or noncooperative if the "word" does not resonate in his spirit.

5. I never belabor a year's theme with insistent mention of it. It is simply "laid on the table" at the inception of the year. That being the case, however, it is very, very striking to note what inevitably happens.

As each year progresses, it is consistently the case that God's hand, moving among the flock, seems over and over to confirm the word. Equally interesting is how, much later in the year, many of the congregation reference the theme and note how it has shaped and brought fruit to their lives.

A Different Approach

I usually do not even inquire of the Lord for a year's theme until sometime in November, but when the "Year of Revelation" focus was given to me so early and so clearly—almost forcibly one day as I was thinking about the Lord's coming—I was very "quickened." Something sparked in my soul. Something stirred a sense of the Holy Spirit's passion to prepare the bride for the Savior's return. Please note: I want to emphasize that He didn't tell me Jesus was coming in that particular calendar year. But I did sense the Lord wanted to come to His people that year with a deeper revelation of Himself and a clearer unfolding of His purpose for them. Thus, with this quickening motivating my quest, I took steps to respond.

1. **I recognized the Lord's desire to manifest a spirit of "revelation" through my pastoral teaching.**

This is consistent with the prayer Paul expresses in Ephesians 1:17, that "the God of our Lord Jesus Christ, the Father of glory, may give to you the spirit of wisdom and revelation in the knowledge of Him [Jesus]." So foundationally, the Year of Revelation became a call for all of us to open to knowing Christ more clearly, dearly and nearly.

2. **I was moved to pursue the Book of Revelation itself, with a strong focus on an unusual priority.**

Rather than the futuristic aspects of the book occupying the primary focus of those studies, I sought to find the practical, pastoral content of Revelation. That aspect of the book is very different from what we pastors have typically pursued. As a rule, this book has not been utilized the same as virtually every other book in the Bible. Almost exclusively, Revelation is reserved for the eschatological rather than the ecclesiological (the "end of time" issues rather than the church in "the here and now").

As a result, it didn't follow the path my usual constraint would have led me to—examining Revelation via a multi-week "verse-by-verse" study. There is merit, of course, in such exposition, an unusual freedom to capture the "Here's how to live now" content—not only the "Here's what to expect in the future." As a result, we focused and embraced newfound riches in Revelation. Naturally, it was unsurprising that we did—isn't it consistent with Jesus' intent in giving the Revelation that we might find practical truth as well as prophetic promise in the Apocalypse?

The discoveries were so meaningful at the personal, daily-life level—the approach so uncommon for a Revelation study—that one of my publishers insisted that videos of the messages be joined to a book, passing on the life principles for today that tend to go unnoticed. They agreed—Revelation is too often relegated in believers' minds to becoming a book of curiosities about the future rather than cures for the present. I've decided that Revelation was never meant to be reserved for specialists in futuristic prophecy. From the beginning of the book, the Savior is found speaking into the day-to-day life of His church. (See Revelation 1:1–3.)

Simply One Example

What I've shared, then, is but a single example of the outflow of the Holy Spirit to this shepherd along the lines of direction He has for the congregation. More occurred, of course, than our being so profitably led into the green pastures of this intriguing book. My practice of seeking a "prophetic word for the year" found fruit in new and similar ways as in other years, and proved again the merit this quest might have for any pastor. In fact, it's consistent with Revelation chapters 2 and 3. In seven cases, Jesus directly addresses the pastors (the "messengers" [angels] to those congregations). Each letter concludes with the same counsel: "If you have an ear to hear, listen to what the Spirit is saying to the churches."

It seems reason enough to believe the same Holy Spirit is equally concerned with speaking to each pastor and flock today. From year to year, it's proven powerfully practical, biblically valid and spiritually fruitful. I encourage this way of leading into each new year. I don't know what the "word" the Spirit gives you may be, but I am sure of two things:

1. It will draw you into the Scriptures and provide discoveries of how God's Word reveals timelessly what He's wanted to emphasize to you and yours at this time.

2. You will realize a very special sense of being a shepherd who is helping his flock more sensitively to hear the Great Shepherd's voice.

When it's all said and done—any year—they are His sheep. That's why I want to hear as clearly as I can what He would like me to relay to them—in His name and from His Word. After all, that's what we're supposed to be up to as shepherds—this year or any year.

Jack Hayford, "A Year of Revelation," *Ministries Today* (January/February 1998): 17-18.

Sharpening Your Leading Edge

Approaching my nation's Independence Day celebration with the banner "Year 2000" theming so many activities, I was asked if I would write a prayer hymn for the occasion. In order that those present not be required to learn a new melody, I wrote these lyrics to "America." It deserves to be retitled yearly (updated from 2000)—sung and prayed.

Toward "America" 2000

Our country, 'tis for thee
We come to intercede
Through Christ our Lord.
Dear Lord, Your promise reads,
You'll heal that land indeed,
When humble hearts confess their need
You will grace afford.

So, God, we come to Thee,
This anniversary
Of our dear land.
Astounded by Your grace
We bow before Your face
To ask, O Lord, that in this place
You extend Your hand.

From pilgrim father's days
We early sought Your ways,
But now confess
As sinful people we
Have turned our back on Thee.
But now this day we make our plea:
God, in mercy, bless.

Bless us with broken hearts,
Repentance, Lord, impart
Into our souls.
Come shatter sinful pride;
Drive back the evil tide.
Where hellish strongholds now reside
Break and make us whole.

Bless us with tears of shame
For we've profaned Your name;
Our lips renew.
Let fiery coals now cleanse
Our tongues, our hearts, our hands,
We praise Your name and take our stand,
Lord, to honor You.

Receive our pledge to fight
By faith against the night
To overcome.

In faith we'll intercede,
Before Your throne we'll plead
Until this land is Yours indeed,
Our home sweet home.

JACK W. HAYFORD

JULY 4, 1999

[chapter 19]   A Nation's Salvation — and Dependence

NONE of us can be sure it will be true indefinitely, but God is speaking to America today. As shepherds charged with leading Jesus' flock, we need to be the first to listen—to keep hope, exercise faith and chart a course of faith-filled action. Our nation's Fourth of July celebration provides a logical season for reviewing both our responsibility and our actions in doing this.

As discouraging as some recent years may have been regarding a decline in the moral and spiritual climate in my country, over the past two years, my faith has been stirred and my convictions steeled: *America can still be saved!* Those words have repeatedly come to my ears—and heart— not only in my personal times of prayer, but as one anointed prophet after another has risen to declare them. Many noted and trusted preachers have sounded the same basic message: *If the living church will rise to be the church God intends, America can be turned around.*

While celebrating her political independence, America's survival, sustenance and salvation are ultimately dependent—and according to God's Word, *the praying, ministering church* is the pivot point upon which it all turns. The power to bring salvation is God's alone. But at the same time, He has indicated that without the invitation issued by the church's intercessions, nothing will change. (See 1 Timothy 2:1–3.) So however seriously imperiled the future of *any* nation may be, it is salvageable, for the Bible reveals that Messiah's seed can turn the day for nations (Ps. 2:8).

I'm not jabbering mere nationalistic small talk or patriotic excitement—I'm trumpeting a prophetic assignment. Together, fellow leaders, our influence holds the potential to determine our nation's destiny.

I've seen it happen before. You would have had to be living in the mid-1970s to know how bleak the social and spiritual situation was in America. Anarchy was at high tide as building burnings and virtual war exploded on many of our nation's college campuses. The Watergate scandal had destroyed the credibility of political leaders and eroded national trust in our government. The struggle over the sustained military action and policies involving us in Vietnam had wrenched the nation's soul with dissension and confusion. Hopelessness prevailed like a cloud over our land, until newspapers raised a question. With the nation's 1976 bicentennial drawing near, they asked, "Will America live to be 200?"

It was at that time that God profoundly called me to lead my congregation in intercession. At first I thought ours was only a local call, but I later discovered that during the same period of time a movement was being born by the Spirit across the country. Believers began to intercede with new power and passion, insight and follow-through action—and God did something mighty! Within a matter of two short years, America's condition, which journalists had likened to the mood preceding our nation's Civil War a century earlier, had been drastically reversed. So much so that in January 1976 the *Washington Post* declared in banner headlines: "A New Spirit Has Come to America!"

People who pray know who that "Spirit" was—the Holy Spirit is the only one who can bring about God's creative, redemptive power at such grand dimensions. And with the approach of every July 4th, I suggest that church leaders remind the people of God of these things. God has brought turnarounds before. When His people pray—healing is available to nations (2 Chron. 7:14). Here are steps to take and ways to lead:

- *First, be caught in the grip of the above promise.* Second Chronicles 7:14-15 is not for poetic, superstitious or sentimental quotation. It's a point of covenant at which our people need to meet God. Lead yours to make it a point of corporate agreement with the Almighty: "Lord, we will take our place—convinced You will take Your place—in releasing redemptive grace."

- *Bless your enemies.* Facing certain distressing aspects of America's behavior has caused some Christians to become "fueled by fury." While pulpit-thumpers are goading many believers to anger, Jesus is calling us to be an answer to our nation—not to be angry with it. "But I say to you, love your enemies...and pray for those who spitefully use you and persecute you" (Matt. 5:44). You can't intercede for a people, nation or political administration with whom you're infuriated.

- *Value life.* Proverbs 31:8 says, "Open your mouth for the speechless, in the cause of all who are appointed to die." Addressing the issues of abortion and euthanasia is not a digression from spiritual concerns. We're at a crisis point in our national experience about whether future generations will value life—at its inception and at its conclusion. But here again, any self-righteous moralizing will only distance us from our society. Instead, may our hearts be broken by the realization that the underlying cause of this sinful devaluation of life is the emptiness of a society that has lost hope for tomorrow.

[■] *Pursue unity.* Mutual respect among all God's redeemed family is absolutely essential if we would win a nation. But such unity requires an end of suspicion, criticism, judgmentalism and all separatism based on ethnic arrogance or doctrinal hair-splitting. Let us resist the voices of those who attack others for the sake of gaining their own following. Jesus' prayer is ours to answer: "That they may all be one…Father…that the world [America!] may know" (John 17:21, 23).

[■] *Live in purity.* The early church showed that the way to assert moral superiority in a corrupt culture is by example, not by taking the role of an adversary. Dear pastors, let's call the church not to *shoot* at society but to *shine* in it. (See Philippians 2:14–15.)

[■] *Serve the needy.* To be in a position to "save" America, the living church must capture the moment amid social need and crisis in our communities. Winning the trust of those we want to reach with Christ's life begins with showing them His love, which can only be done through serving. Jesus said that good works create a platform for the gospel. (See Matthew 5:16.)

[■] *Preserve liberty.* I lament the preoccupation some American Christians have with changing our nation through a political agenda alone. Without first laying a foundation in prayer, love and good works, their otherwise worthy goals have a clanging sound.

However, the preservation of America's liberty does necessitate taking certain action. Our participation in the political privileges of our free society is the responsible exercise of our role as disciples of Jesus.

- *Finally, let's evangelize!* The only way a nation can be saved is if souls are saved. To leave this until last is not to diminish its importance, but to accentuate it. And it's also to make clear that our gospel will be more readily received and believed if we've done the other things first—then let's demonstrate, declare and dispense the gospel.

Some people think spiritual leaders are entrusted only with the task of, on occasion, prophesying a nation's doom. But there is an earlier task—that of calling God's people to faith, obedience, prayerful intercession and godly action. In that light, there is reason to embrace the persuasion that a glorious crossroads of possibility is at hand. A sovereign visitation is always possible—even in the worse situation. Where sin abounds, grace may much more abound (Rom. 5:20).

America's Fourth of July is a fitting time for American church leaders to be renewed in that conviction.

Jack Hayford, "Steps to Save America," *Ministries Today* (July/August 1995): 24–25.

Conclusion

It was a beleaguered leader who wrote the words. Words wrapped in the middle of a series of letters now bunched into one we call 2 Corinthians.

Words written to some people he had loved and led. Who were *forgetting* now:

> [■] **Forgetting *him*, though he'd laid himself out for them.**

And worse:

> [■] **Forgetting so much of *Jesus'* heart. And He had died for them.**

The leader's words were passion-filled. Written with little of his usual logic. They weren't incoherent or disorganized, just mixed with tears. Sometimes. And other times, with impassioned pleas for understanding. For their sake.

Then the letter turned a corner: "I'm not losing heart, even though so much around and about me is wearing out. Fading like overused fabric. Wilting like sunburnt grass."

There were more words to come, but these have spoken to

my heart. Often. To you, too? Maybe even now?

So often we all feel that way.

Not because we're whimperers or whiners. Only because leaders are human, and because making a difference for God, with people, takes time. And tears. And pain. And sometimes without seeing that a lasting deposit is being made, even amid our frail, seemingly failed efforts.

Little surprise, however. The same thing happened with our Leader. He said:

> **If the world hates you, you know that it hated Me before it hated you...Most assuredly, I say to you, a servant is not greater than his master; nor is he who is sent greater than he who sent him.**

> —John 15:18; 13:16

So, as leaders He has appointed, we are drawn to the case study above; to the words of Paul—wearied with the battle, harried by the church in Corinth.

But don't miss the punch line. Be sure and read *all* his words. Because at that point he began by admitting his fading strength, he finishes with a declaration: He concludes: "Whatever has been perishing is being renewed—every day!"

And more:

> Therefore we do not lose heart. Even though our outward man is perishing, yet the inward man is being renewed day by day. For our light affliction, which is but for a moment, is working for us a far more exceeding and eternal weight of glory.
>
> —2 Corinthians 4:16–17

So I leave you with that, dear reader. I end now, noting the doubly great promise inherent in this one episode from God's eternal Word:

- First, that an eternal arm will sustain and renew us, however worn or wearied we may be—however misunderstood or disregarded.

- Second, that whatever we do will *last*; that the actions of *months or moments*, however transient, have the seeds of "glory-weight" in them. That thereby, God's own glory infuses our weakest efforts. That what you and I do in Jesus' name, however weak we feel, is invested with something of Himself. Something that will leave a lasting deposit. Beyond our weakness, glory-weight. He says so.

So, take the promise. Stay the course. Fight faith's fight. Glory all the way.

For Glory-Weight, O Lord

I come to You, O Lord my God,
  To seek Your grace and strength;
That I may please Your heart this day,
  And serve Your will at length.
That every word I speak may bless;
  Each soul I touch may feel,
That my dear Savior passed their way—
  Incarnate—live and real.

So with my everydays, my God
  (Some bright, some overcast)
I pray whate'er the climate be
  That all I do will last.
Let substance fill my words and deeds;
  With glory-weight endow
Each transient moment that I live—
  Reveal an eternal now.

—JACK W. HAYFORD

Notes

1. Jack W. Hayford, *How to Live Through a Bad Day* (Nashville, TN: Thomas Nelson, 2001).

2. Material on the "Eight Biblical Principles of Reconciliation" is available at the PromiseKeepers website at www.promisekeepers.org. You can also contact them at P. O. Box 103001, Denver, CO 80250-3001. Their general information phone number is 800-888-7595.

3. Don Finto, *Your People Shall Be My People* (Ventura, CA: Regal Books, 2001).

4. Daniel Juster, *Israel, the Church and the Last Days* (Shippensburg, PA: Destiny Image, 1990). Daniel Juster, *Jewish Roots* (Shippensburg, PA: Destiny Image, 1995).

5. Jack Deere, *Surprised by the Power of the Spirit* (Grand Rapids, MI: Zondervan, 1993).

6. Che Ahn, ed., *Hosting the Holy Spirit* (Ventura, CA: Regal Books, 2000).

7. Dallas Willard, *The Spirit of the Disciplines* (San Francisco: Harper San Francisco, 1991). Richard Foster, *Celebration of Discipline* (San Francisco: Harper San Francisco, 1988).

8. Jack W. Hayford, *Living the Spirit-Formed Life* (Ventura, CA: Regal Books, 2001).

9. Jack W. Hayford, *Pastors of Promise* (Ventura, CA: Regal Books, 1997).

10. Jack W. Hayford, The Power to Become series (Nashville, TN: Thomas Nelson, 1995). A six-volume set including *A Man's Starting Place, A Man's Confidence, A Man's Walk With God, A Man's Image and Identity, A Man's Integrity*

and *A Man's Worship and Witness.*

11. Jack W. Hayford, *A Passion for Fullness* (Nashville, TN: Word, 1990).

12. Jack W. Hayford, *Grounds for Living* (n.p.: Sovereign World, Ltd., 2001).

13. Rebecca Hayford Bauer, *The 25 Days of Christmas* (n.p.: Chariot Victor Books, 1999).

14. Rebecca Hayford Bauer, *Seasons of Praise* (n.p.: Chariot Victor Pub., 1996).

Get Grounded *in the Word*
with Pastor Jack

Explore some of the biblical resources produced under Dr. Hayford's writing and editorial leadership:

Dr. Jack Hayford, Founder, The King's College & Seminary

The New Spirit-Filled Life Bible
The insight-filled study Bible has already provided prophetic and practical help for 1.5 million growing believers

Spirit-Filled Life Study Guides
38 separate 100+-page interactive studies focusing on individual books of the Bible, plus topical studies providing practical application of important spiritual principles

Hayford's Bible Handbook
A study resource that uniquely unveils "Kingdom Keys" to Scripture; a wealth of valuable information and a spiritual stimulus that will encourage faith, growth and Spirit-filled service to Christ as you explore His Word

For more information on these or other helpful resources by Jack Hayford, visit www.jackhayford.com. There you may:

- Purchase from over 40 books and 1500 tapes by Jack Hayford, including:
  - *Worship His Majesty, The Beauty of Spiritual Language*
  - *A Passion for Fullness, Living the Spirit-Formed Life*
- Listen to the Living Way Ministries radio and television program
- Receive information about Dr. Hayford's upcoming events

— and —

- Investigate The King's College and Seminary, founded by Dr. Jack Hayford
  - Call **1-888-779-8040** for more information about this rapidly growing center equipping Word-centered, Spirit-filled leaders.
  - Undergraduate and graduate programs (recognized by the U.S. Department of Education, TRACS and AABC) are available through online, on-campus and modular intensive formats.
  - **The Jack W. Hayford School of Pastoral Nurture** is a 6-day interactive intensive with Pastor Hayford for the continued education and enrichment of senior pastors from all backgrounds.

14800 Sherman Way, Van Nuys, CA 91405 • 888-779-8040 • www.jackhayford.com

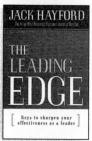

Your Walk With God Can Be Even Deeper...

With *Charisma* magazine, you'll be informed and inspired by the features and stories about what the Holy Spirit is doing in the lives of believers today.

Each issue:
- Brings you exclusive world-wide reports to rejoice over.
- Keeps you informed on the latest news from a Christian perspective.
- Includes miracle-filled testimonies to build your faith.
- Gives you access to relevant teaching and exhortation from the most respected Christian leaders of our day.

Call 1-800-829-3346 for 3 FREE trial issues
Offer #A2CCHB

If you like what you see, then pay the invoice of $22.97 (**saving over 51% off the cover price**) and receive 9 more issues (12 in all). Otherwise, write "cancel" on the invoice, return it, and owe nothing.

Experience the Power of Spirit-Led Living